"I trust John Elmore. He li church. Revival is a hard t growing devotion to the L fire God will start in you as pages of this book. It's a fire our world is craving and one I hope spreads to the ends of the earth. Churches must become hospitals. And John Elmore is the one to lead such a movement."

Jennie Allen, New York Times bestselling author of *Get Out of Your Head*; founder and visionary of IF:Gathering

"I am a John Elmore fan! Over the years I have been inspired by John's candor about his struggle with addiction and his journey to freedom. He has walked the road of recovery and helped countless others do the same. I am thrilled that he has put a resource in our hands that can help all of us!"

Ben Stuart, pastor of Passion City Church DC; author of *Single, Dating, Engaged, Married*

"Jesus is all we need. I sing it all the time. 'Who do I have in heaven but you?' And yet I fall way short! At times I crave and run after things of the world. And every once in a while, a book like this comes along and helps unpack how to take advantage of the resource that is ours in Christ. How to cash in the eternal chips of our inheritance. How to return to and enjoy our First Love over all things. I have had the privilege of walking in community with John over the last few years, and I can honestly say the freedom in Christ to which I have had a front-row seat by walking with him is now also yours. Drink deep— one day at a time. Let's go!"

Shane Barnard, singer/songwriter for Shane & Shane and shaneandshane.com

"Over the past decade, I've personally witnessed God use John Elmore to set prisoners free by the thousands. He is, quite literally, the best pastor I know. The methods in *Freedom Starts Today* are proven, effective ways to help *anyone* walk in the abundant life that Jesus promises. If you are wondering if this book is for you, I assure you that it will be an amazing journey you don't want to miss out on. Freedom, indeed, starts the second you begin reading."

Jonathan Pokluda, bestselling author of *Welcome to Adulting*; host of *Becoming Something* podcast; pastor of Harris Creek in Waco, TX

"It has been said, 'We often underestimate what we can do in a week and overestimate what we can do in a year.' In *Freedom Starts Today*, John Elmore dismisses long-range planning and big-dream visioning in favor of a focus on your next 24 hours. What can you do today? Whether you have a small struggle or an overwhelming addiction,

John's daily entries will bring focus and freedom to your life day by day. Don't delay. Start today."

"*Freedom Starts Today* is a clarion call for believers succumbed by secret sin—from porn to pride and everything in between—to find the freedom and deep fellowship promised in Christ. This book is a practical lifeline to freedom."

"Every year, John Elmore comes and teaches our young adults about the power of God over sin in their lives. The resulting fruit of the Spirit is sanctification seen in surrender, confession of sin, repentance, and freedom to live the full, abundant life Jesus promised. As I told John when he was just a couple of months sober, "The soil is most fertile in the valleys." Begin your journey with God through *Freedom Starts Today*, and your valley will soon become Christ's victory."

"Whether our issues are pain or shame, *Freedom Starts Today* is a reliable ninety-day roadmap to real freedom in Christ. This book by John Elmore is refreshingly honest, personally convicting, creative, and engaging. The quotations and daily accountability exercises alone are worth the price. This is a book to read and then recommend."

"My husband and I have had the privilege of being friends with John Elmore for years. We've seen him on- and offstage. I can say with absolute integrity that he practices what he preaches. He is driven by the wholehearted conviction that Jesus changes everything, and with God, all things are possible—even the impossible. I am confident the Holy Spirit will use this book to liberate many who never thought it possible."

"John Elmore is one of my favorite people. When he speaks, I listen. When he lives, I learn. When he writes, I read. You may not get to hear him or see him, but I am glad you can read what he has to share about the hope of Christ's transforming power and the life that awaits all who come weary and heavy-laden. Dive in, read well, and live free!"

FREEDOM STARTS TODAY

FREEDOM STARTS TODAY

Overcoming Struggles
and Addictions
One Day at a Time

JOHN ELMORE

BakerBooks
a division of Baker Publishing Group
www.BakerBooks.com

Published by Baker Books
a division of Baker Publishing Group
PO Box 6287, Grand Rapids, MI 49516–6287
www.bakerbooks.com

Printed in the United States of America

Library of Congress Cataloging-in-Publication Data
Names: Elmore, John, 1975– author.
Title: Freedom starts today : overcoming struggles and addictions one day at a time / John Elmore.
Description: Grand Rapids, Michigan : Baker Books, a division of Baker Publishing Group, 2021.
Identifiers: LCCN 2020024593 | ISBN 9781540900623 (paperback) | ISBN 9781540901446 (casebound)
Subjects: LCSH: Addicts—Religious life—Miscellanea. | Substance abuse—Religious aspects—Christianity—Miscellanea. | Habit breaking—Religious aspects—Christianity—Miscellanea. | Sins—Miscellanea. | Sin—Christianity—Miscellanea. | Spiritual exercises.
Classification: LCC BV4596.A24 E45 2021 | DDC 248.8/629—dc23
LC record available at https://lccn.loc.gov/2020024593

The proprietor is represented by the literary agency of The Gates Group.

21 22 23 24 25 26 27   7 6 5 4 3 2

This book is dedicated to you,

_____,

(Write your name here)

and to the eradication of addiction in the church.

(Submit your information at
freedomstartstoday.org;
I will pray for you.)

Contents

Contents

Acknowledgments

WITH LIFELONG GRATITUDE TO:

My Laura—thank you for saying yes. You are Christ's tangible grace to me. I love walking Home with you.

Hill, Penny, and Judd—you are my proof that God does not treat us as our sins deserve. I'm so proud of you and thankful to be your dad.

Mom, Dad, Matt, and Mandy—thank you for a lifetime of encouragement, your intervening love when life was unraveling, and all the support in the years of rebuilding.

Charlie P.—for holding my hand the first three months of life without alcohol and teaching me the power of daily sobriety by God's strength.

Keith Chancey and Chad Hampsch—for your discipleship that Jesus used to reshape my heart, mind, and life and for your Hebrews 13:7 lives.

Dr. Scott Horrell—thank you for teaching me with God-honoring passion the glory, work, and roles of the Father, Son, and Spirit.

Dr. Paul Pettit—thank you for discipling me, loving me, and graciously entrusting leadership to this former liability.

Rick and Linda Jo Strickland—thank you for loving me in my present and not caring about my past.

Watermark Community Church—thank you for taking a chance on an old drunk made new in Christ and for the years you've spent investing in me.

My brothers and sisters of re:generation—you lead the church in surrender unto sanctification, and your lives are pages out of the Gospels. Every Monday you are my Romans 1:12.

The Barnards, Frizzells, Pokludas, and Treadaways—living out the one-anothers of Scriptures with you and our children has been the richest gift.

And to Don Gates of The Gates Group (my incredible advocate and agent), Rebekah Guzman, Amy Ballor, Nicci Jordan Hubert, Abby Van Wormer, Patti Brinks, Melanie Burkhardt, Erin Bartels, Rachel O'Connor, Janelle Wiesen, and the entire Baker Publishing Group team—you all work tirelessly to put into people's hands the transforming truths of God and do so on a world-class level. It's an honor to serve with you.

Introduction

I PUT A SHOTGUN TO MY HEAD because I wanted my life to end. I wanted the pain to be over. And I wondered if I could go through with it.

It was September 2005, and I was losing everything, including my sanity. I could feel the darkness around me. Insomnia, mania, nightmares, loss of appetite, risky behavior. I had three doctors tell me I would die if I kept drinking. I thought, *Good. I want to die but don't want to hurt my family by committing suicide. But I hope one morning I just don't wake up.* I drank hard for twelve years straight and was a functional alcoholic. What an ironic justification: "Congrats! You are a total drunk who can hold down a job."

After the horrific end of a relationship, I became a dysfunctional alcoholic trying to numb the pain. Three months later, on a Wednesday morning, I was drinking with two homeless guys in Austin, Texas. I was so lonely. I told them to come sit with me and I would buy them whatever they wanted. This was a new low for me, and my family knew it. Five hundred dollars and eight hours later, my big brother was on a one-way flight to Austin to put me in my own car and take me to Dallas for a family intervention.

I walked into my first twelve-step recovery meeting five days later. It was the scariest thing I've ever done. But what happened that night, and the things that followed, changed the rest of my life.

I was set free—and that's why I've now written this book for you and others who long for freedom. The principles and practices of this book are what God used to walk me out of an addiction that was killing me. I have personally witnessed porn addicts, same-sex strugglers, sex addicts, alcoholics, drug addicts, codependents, and more be set free by what (or more accurately Who) you'll encounter in this book.

And yet this is *not* a book; it's a daily journey—for *you*. This isn't a normal book, where you just read what I have written but don't interact with the material. Instead, it contains daily entries for daily freedom from struggles, as well as opportunities to journal, pray, live out what you've learned, and be held accountable throughout. So don't worry—your journey to freedom begins just a couple of pages from here, *not* after reading through this whole book. Freedom starts today.

The principles within are applicable to all sin struggles. Two years ago, while on a date night with my wife, Laura, she said, "I just wish we wouldn't fight anymore for the rest of our lives." In that moment, I thought, *God was powerful enough to free you from alcoholism. Surely He can free you from quarreling with your wife.* So I started employing the practices in this book in my marriage to stop bickering with Laura. Guess what? We got into three arguments that year. If you're married, you *know* that's a miracle. Ever since, we don't fight like we used to (and I'm the only one who changed anything, which implicates me as the main source of the problem). Now I'm asking God to help me stop being short and sharp with my kids when they disobey, and I believe God's power will free me from those harsh moments with my children as well.

Sin is a supernatural problem that demands a supernatural answer. You have no power over sin; God has all power over it. So if you're tired of losing the fight against sin, prepare to no longer be tired. You feel this way because you have been fighting a more powerful foe. This book will help you learn how to bring God into the fight, for as Jesus said, "Come to me, all who labor and are heavy laden, and I will give you rest" (Matt. 11:28).

One of the Holy Spirit's main roles (and often most overlooked role) in our lives is to kill sin and make us like Jesus (sanctify us), but we neglect Him. We know and talk a lot about the fruit of the Spirit, the good things He bears in our lives, but we don't talk as much about the "negative work" of the Holy Spirit. This sounds strange, doesn't it? How could anything God does be negative? It's not. The great theologian John Owen, in his book *Of the Mortification of Sin in Believers*, calls the negative work of the Holy Spirit His warring against sin on our behalf. He both produces positive fruit in us and kills the negative sin within us. So, as for this exhausting wrestle with sin? Not anymore. God lives to set His children free; we need only to ask and depend on Him.

To set up this premise of *daily* warring against sin by the Spirit, it's important to know this isn't some new fad or a Christianese life hack to quit sin. This is how the church has always warred against sin, but we have forgotten. This is nothing new, but it will make you new. Martin Luther, the great Reformer who brought the gospel back to the church, wrote his 95 Theses. And the first four, implying they were of utmost importance, centered on repentance. Here are theses 1 and 3: "When our Lord and Master Jesus Christ said, 'Repent' [Matt. 4:17], he willed the entire life of believers to be one of repentance. Yet it does not mean solely inner repentance; such inner repentance is worthless unless it produces various outward mortification of the flesh."[1] And again, Owen, in

Of the Mortification of Sin in Believers, asks of the church, "Do you mortify [sin]; do you make it your daily work; be always at it [while] you live; cease not a day from this work; be killing sin or it will be killing you."[2] Jonathan Edwards was also grounded on daily repentance, which birthed his list of resolutions—seventy things he willed to do and not do. He would read these weekly to remind himself of advancing the kingdom and subduing the flesh. And God used the application of these bold truths to set the church on fire.

So now it's your turn to consider what they did: What will you daily ask Him to free you from?

Freedom Starts Today will walk you into freedom from your struggle or addiction in 24 hours, one day at a time, indefinitely. If you go all in, the next ninety days will be life altering, sin destroying, and God glorifying. You see, God said that anyone who has trusted in Christ is no longer a slave to sin. The jail cell has been unlocked and the door is open, but ironically, we stay put. It is familiar; we actually kind of love what we hate. But I know and you know that if you're reading this, it's because you're ready for freedom. And if this freedom-in-Christ thing is actually true, actually lasting, actually available, then you're listening.

And I would not waste my time or yours if the daily practice and promises in this book weren't completely true for every single person who trusts in Jesus. Once Jesus did what He did for me fifteen years ago, I decided I would spend the rest of my life telling people that Jesus is real, they're never too far gone, and He can change everything.

Who This Book Is For: People Struggling with Sin or an Addiction

(By the way, everyone struggles with sin or an addiction. Yes, even your pastor. How do I know? I am a pastor and I know many.)

This book is for the church—because the church is addicted. Let that sink in. The very body and bride of Christ is addicted. *Every* church has *many* people addicted to porn, pills, control/anxiety, social media, food/body image, work/status/money, self-harm, alcohol, codependency, sexual impurity, and more. But there are many more socially acceptable sins that are just as spiritually lethal: pride, gossip, workaholism, materialism, and others. I believe you are reading this because you want to be free from something in your life. Something you've tried to quit, stop, or get rid of but keeps coming back around. And I have comforting news to quiet some of the shame: so does everyone else. Your mom, your boss, your neighbor, your spouse, your waiter, your pastor, everyone. Everyone has something in their life that shouldn't be there; it's the human condition this side of heaven.

We have ignored addiction for too long because it's too big, too awful, too pervasive, and seemingly too impossible to cure. And if the church doesn't have the antidote to sin, our faith is a joke. But our faith is not a joke, because, in fact, we do have the Antidote, the only antidote to sin. As Jesus becomes more in your life, sin will become less. It is Christ's will to eradicate sin and addiction from the church (Eph. 5:25–27), and He will sanctify His bride, one person at a time, one struggle at a time, one day at a time. This book makes clear and simple the path to freedom from sin struggles by the power of the Holy Spirit in the context of community. This book is not going to unpack the science or theology of addiction; odds are you don't need convincing of the how or why of addiction. I believe you just want to be free. I know I did.

Sin, Satan, and years of defeat have left people believing that God's power isn't potent enough for their personal sin. They may be saved eternally but have resolved that they will have to eke out a life of spiritual defeat against sin in this life. Many are also being told that if they just had enough faith or hatred for sin, they would be healed and freed. Thus, it is either God's problem or their problem, yet either way, the problem remains.

To that end, this is not a theological, psychological, or bio-medical treatise on sin and addiction; addicts and strugglers don't have time for that. Neither is it a fiery brimstone rebuke; Jesus simply wouldn't have that. This is sin-shattering orthodoxy (right beliefs) translated to life-changing orthopraxy (right living) on every page for every day, because though the war is won, the battles are relentless. You don't need 24 chapters about addiction or inspirational feels; you need to be struggle-free in the next 24 hours. This book focuses on that, because God delivers on His promises. Every. Single. Time.

To say that a book will deliver people from addiction in 24 hours is an alarmingly big and a ridiculously boastful promise, unless it's not about the book. This book lays plain the way of personal appropriation of God's promises offered to each of us in the Scriptures. This is done through Jesus by the power of the Holy Spirit and the healing found in confession to and encouragement by the body of Christ. Make no mistake: there is no power in *Freedom Starts Today*. The power is in God and living out the Scriptural principles and promises of God each day. As you pray in daily surrender, live in daily community, and walk out these ninety promises and truths of God, He alone can and will set you free. We are told in 1 Peter 1:2 that the Holy Spirit is the Sanctifier and in Romans 8:13 that the Spirit kills sin. Thus, to live the promised full, abundant, victorious life, we *must* bring Him into the fight—*daily*.

This book leads you on a path of Spirit-empowered daily repentance and mines the Scriptures for divinely grand promises, unpacking them with illustrations to aid in understanding and memory. It also includes journaling space for a prayer, as well as a daily proactive commitment, by God's strength and with another person, to sobriety from a sin for the next 24 hours. This is not reactive confession of sin after it's already happened. Similar to Jonathan Edwards's resolutions, this is a proactive decision by God's strength not to give in to a particular sin.

Everyone would love not to give in to their struggle for the rest of their lives, but that feels like an impossible Everest. So, don't. Determine to quit for one, singular, infinitely more feasible day. Because while no one could climb Everest in a day, everyone could advance one step. That is all God asks—a daily walk with Him. The strategy and reality of conquering the mountain of sin is by advancing one day at a time (Gal. 5:16). To say it personally, I haven't been sober for fifteen years; I've been sober for 5,475 days. Victory over sin is found one day at a time, and the victory is won by Jesus.

People often ask me about their respective addictions and how to stop. I reply, "If I asked you to quit for the rest of your life, would you be able?" They hang their head in despair or shame and say something like "No. I wish I could, but history would say otherwise." Then I ask what I was asked at my first Alcoholics Anonymous meeting: "Well, do you think, by God's strength, you could stay sober for 24 hours?" When I ask that question, the answer is a resounding and eager yes. So, we do just that, together. Surrender, repentance, and accountability win the daily war against sin, and a new life is wrought.

In Christianity, most often (if ever) we confess sin reactively. That is, *after* the sin has already been committed. Reactive confession is good, biblical, and right, but at the same time, the sin has already happened. If you want to overcome addictive behavior, waiting until the behavior has occurred yet again can leave you feeling stuck in a defeating cycle. But what if you both confessed your sin *and* decided to go on the offensive (the theological term is *repent*, or a turning from sin by turning toward God)? We do this by making a *proactive* decision by God's strength not to do/use/say/go/act upon "xyz" over the next 24 hours. Then, let another person know about your commitment, and plan to follow up with them 24 hours later and let them know if you abstained. Then, when temptation inevitably comes during that period, you remember your commitment that you'll have to follow up with your friend the next day (your resolve is strengthened), you pray more (become dependent on God), you reach out to your brother/sister in Christ for help (they pray and encourage you). After 24 hours, you call or text and tell them if you stayed free from whatever struggle and also make another proactive commitment of 24 hours free from that struggle by God's strength. You follow up again after another 24 hours, commit again, and repeat this daily.

In this way, I've seen so many people freed from addiction, both in our church's recovery program and other programs, like AA. When I was first getting sober, I would remember I'd have to call Charlie the next day and let him know whether or not I stayed sober. That communal aspect of my recovery, knowing I'd be checking in with someone, was pivotal and strengthened my decision not to drink that day.

Traditionally, as people war against sin and fall, they feel "it" didn't work and give up trying. Instead, *Freedom Starts Today* teaches a new way of living: regardless of falling, the answer is daily repentance. It's time recovery circles and rehabs aren't the only places sin is being proactively warred against and struggles being overcome. The church should be leading and winning the war. And if so, the church universal will see healing, transformation, mission-minded members, and deep fellowship flood back into its body through confession, daily repentance, discipleship, biblical community, and a powerful living out of Scripture. This is the will of God. And

He delights to fulfill His will. We need only ask, and we will receive. May it be so.

As such, this is not a book of God's promises; the world has enough of those. Nor is it a daily devotional; same story. This is a practical, immediately applicable methodology of learning to war against sin daily while providing a powerful promise of God or a transforming truth for each day.

I am a recovering alcoholic. I was a drunk for twelve years and now have been sober for fifteen. And this book, this journey, will walk you through the same path of getting free from an addiction that God used to set me free, and that I've seen so many others use. It's simple. It's powerful. It's the gospel. And it's for you.

How to Use This Book: Daily Readings, Daily Prayer Journaling, and Daily Commitments

When you're addicted to or struggling with something, you don't have time to read a three-hundred-page book, you need immediate, effective help. As such, this is not a "read it cover to cover" book. It's a book of daily entries that will take only about ten minutes per day for ninety days in a row. It requires your personal interaction and commitment, and a faithful brother or sister in Christ to journey along with you or it'll be a waste of your time. And this book is not a substitute for what the Bible puts forth as the Christian life; it is a supplement with helpful tracks to run on. As such, in addition to going through this book, be in church weekly, go deep with a small group throughout the week, read the Bible, memorize Scripture, and pray daily—live a life of worship.

How long does it take to break a bad habit? Previous psychology has said twenty-one days. More recent research says sixty-six days. Good news: God says that if we will walk with Him *today*, we will not do the things we don't want to do (Gal.

5:16). That's an incredible promise. Our command is simply to walk with Him one day at a time. Then He gives that crazy, life-altering promise: you won't gratify the desires of the flesh. Walking with Him keeps you from walking back down that regrettable path we all have. Forget hoping for twenty-one or sixty-six days; in Christ, freedom starts today!

Here's how it works and what it entails (10 minutes total each day):

1. **Read** a story based on Scripture that unpacks that spiritual truth (*2 minutes*).

2. **Write** a prayer to God about what you've learned, and ask Him to transform you by the truth you've just read (*2 minutes*).

3. **Pray** and ask God to keep you from your addiction for the next 24 hours *by His strength*. This is key: make sure your commitment to 24-hour sobriety is by *His* strength. Pray in a humble position (arms raised, on your knees, etc.). FYI, I have prayed on my knees with my face to the floor almost every day for the past fifteen years, and I believe it has been so good to humbly begin each day in a position of glad submission before my King. If you're able, I recommend you do the same each day (*2 minutes*).

4. **Text or call** a trusted Christian friend and tell them you've committed to being sober from your struggle/ addiction for the next 24 hours, by God's strength, and that you will follow up with them the next day to let them know if you stayed free from it (*1 minute*).

   • That's it. Text or call and say, "Hey, _____, I commit to you, by God's strength, not to _____ for the next 24 hours. And tomorrow at this time, I'll follow up with you to let you know how I did. Will you please pray for me?"

- The next day, at that same time, follow up with your friend and let them know how you did (set an alarm on your phone as a reminder to text your friend). Then commit to them to abstain, by God's strength, from _____ again for another 24 hours.
- And repeat that pattern indefinitely. It's your daily path to freedom—all by God's strength, His Word, and the support of His people.
- Remember, you can't do this alone. As it's been said, illness starts with an *I* and wellness begins with *we*. God has designed the Christian life that no one can get healthy and free and healed alone. To attempt this alone is contrary to the will of God found in James 5:16: "Therefore confess your sins to each other and pray for each other so that you may be healed" (NIV).

5. **Read** the suggested chapter of Scripture, as God's Word promises that it will be sanctifying for you (John 17:17) (*3 minutes*).

Why Do This? Why *Freedom Starts Today?*

Satan has sold you a false bill of goods. You may have trusted in Jesus for eternal salvation but are not experiencing daily salvation—here on this side of eternity, you have succumbed to defeat in one or even a few areas. Satan whispers in a voice that sounds all too much like your own, "This is just your lot in life. It's who you are. If God really loved you, He would have taken away these desires. You've struggled with this for a decade or more, and nothing will ever change. You've asked God to save you from this struggle and He hasn't, which means you don't have enough faith or He doesn't have enough power or concern." The lies are just that: lies. The truth is, God longs to see you free and set you free. It doesn't matter how long your thing has been your thing; Christ will set you free. He lived, died, and rose again for that truth and for you to live in the reality of that freedom found in Him alone. And this won't be a focus on sin (that doesn't help anything); this is a focus on Christ (who heals everything). It's replacing an addiction of sin with your affection for Him—a growing love of Christ crowding out the lust for sin.

Don't believe the lies another day. Christ has better for you. He freed me from what I couldn't free myself from. *This isn't* a self-help book, power-of-positive-thinking garbage, or how to do something by new habits and previously untapped willpower. *This is* personally appropriating the power and promises of God and infusing them into your daily life. You walk with God, and God does the work. Period. There is no other way.

These bold claims you've read are straight from Scripture. They're not ripped out of context. It's not prosperity gospel. It's not spiritual psychobabble. It's the true gospel, founded on the Holy Scriptures, empowered by the Holy Spirit, and lived out with the body of Christ.

This is about a proactive, daily decision to war against sin, based on the power of God and the encouragement of God's people. Proactive. Power. People. That's what God will use to set you free. Aren't you ready to be free?

Pick a Fight and a Person

Some people think they don't really have a struggle. That's just a lack of self-awareness. We all have our ditches, our things we run to or fall prey to when life's pressures and pleasures are calling.

So, pray this: "Search me, O God, and know my heart! Try me and know my thoughts! And see if there be any grievous way in me, and lead me in the way everlasting!" (Ps. 139:23–24). Pray and ask God which struggle He would have you war against first.

Really, stop and pray. Ask Him.

Then prepare yourself for battle.

And if you fall, fall forward, kneeling in confession of sin. Ask God to give you freedom one day at a time (one hour at a time, if necessary) in surrender to your Master and in humble thanksgiving, being certain that He isn't mad at you, He loves you, and He longs to walk with you daily.

> For the righteous falls seven times and rises again. (Prov. 24:16)

Now that you've chosen which struggle to war against, you need to pick a person to journey with. Choose someone of the same gender who is a faithful Christ-follower (ideally from your home church). And don't bounce around from person to person; prayerfully choose someone and go deep.

And now, let's begin. One day at a time. And may the war against sin start today. As you read, each day's entry will have a powerful promise or transformational truth from God to you. These aren't just general truths; they are true for *you*. Remember this:

> For all the promises of God find their Yes in him [Jesus]. That is why it is through him that we utter our Amen to God for his glory. (2 Cor. 1:20)

THE END

(of warring against sin
by your own strength and losing)

Then he said to me, "This is what the LORD says . . . :
It is not by force nor by strength, but by my Spirit,
says the LORD of Heaven's Armies. . . .
Do not despise these small beginnings,
for the LORD rejoices to see the work begin."
(Zech. 4:6, 10 NLT)

DAILY ENTRIES

DAY 1

Sober 24 Hours

The nature of Christ's salvation is woefully misrepresented by the present-day "evangelist." He announces a Saviour from Hell rather than a Saviour from sin. And that is why so many are fatally deceived, for there are multitudes who wish to escape the Lake of fire who have no desire to be delivered from their carnality and worldliness.

A. W. Pink

CHARLIE P., MY AA SPONSOR, asked me a question the first night I met him that changed the rest of my life. This question has shaped the way I help other strugglers and addicts. He asked me if I could stay sober from alcohol for one day with God's strength. I told him I needed serious help; I didn't need one day of sobriety. In the past, I'd been sober for a weekend, a week, and one time even a month. I needed real help, not some stupid 24-hour commitment. But I finally gave in. I committed by God's strength not to drink for 24 hours. I knelt beside the couch I was living on and begged God to help me. I checked in with Charlie the next day, still telling him I needed something more. He persisted and I relented. Another 24 hours. Then seven days in a row. Then a month. Then three months. I was feeling seriously free. And now it's been fifteen years. I don't call Charlie every day anymore, but I'm still every bit as dependent daily on God. I still kneel and surrender every single day to the Lord. Something about being in that position of humility and asking Him to lead my day puts things in the right perspective and helps me see that He is a really good Lord of my life (and I am not).

In *The Magician's Nephew*, one of the books in C. S. Lewis's The Chronicles of Narnia, the children are wondering if Aslan would not have realized they would need food for their journey. "'Wouldn't he know without being asked?' said Polly. 'I've no doubt he would,' said the Horse (still with his mouth full). 'But I've a sort of an idea he likes to be asked.'"[1] In much the same way, does God know that you need to be freed from your addiction and struggle? Absolutely. Does it honor Him and keep you in daily dependence to ask Him every day? Absolutely, all the more. And so we do.

Now it's your turn; it's day one of your journey.

So I'll ask you what Charlie asked me on December 27, 2005:

> Would you, by God's strength, commit to not
> _____ for the next 24 hours?
>
> _____ (Yes or No)

This daily dependence on God for freedom is from Matthew 6:33–34:

> But seek first the kingdom of God and his righteousness, and all these things will be added to you. Therefore do not be anxious about tomorrow, for tomorrow will be anxious for itself. Sufficient for the day is its own trouble.

Write a prayer below asking God to help you keep from your struggle today and thanking Him for his power and righteousness.

_____

_____

_____

_____

_____

_____

_____

In a position of humility, pray and ask God to keep you from your struggle for the next 24 hours.

Text or call a brother or sister in Christ to let them know you're committing, by God's strength, to staying free from your struggle/addiction for the next 24 hours and you'll follow up with them tomorrow to let them know if you did.

Example text: "I'm committing to you, by God's strength, that I won't look at porn for the next 24 hours. And I'll follow up with you at this time tomorrow and let you know if I stayed free."

Once you have done so, initial here: ___ Date: _____

» SCRIPTURE READING: Matthew 6

DAY 2

The Power of a Penny

None can become fit for the future life, who hath not practiced himself for it now.

St. Augustine

IT'S EASY TO THINK PENNIES don't matter. They are free for the taking at some cash registers to help make change. People don't even pick up pennies when they see them lying on the ground. They're negligible and seen as almost worthless. Yet no matter who the richest person in the US is or ever will be, their wealth, if you broke it down, would be amassed of single cents. The billionaire, in a very real sense, just has tons of pennies. Ironic, isn't it? One penny is seen as borderline worthless. But an accumulation of them could be a fortune.

Struggles and addictions can feel like this. One day of freedom or sobriety? So what? That's not worth much. But just as a rich person's wealth is made of single cents, a lifetime of freedom is made up of single days. Two things about my sobriety: First, as I said earlier, I'm not fifteen years sober from alcoholism; I'm 5,475 days sober. My sobriety has come one single day at a time and so will yours. There is no other way. But that's good news. I'm not asking you to stay sober for a thousand days in a row—just one day, by God's strength. Second, sometimes when people ask, "How long have you been sober?" I say, "Well, it's almost 2:00 p.m., so I've been sober about eight hours." Meaning, all that matters is that I'm sober today, walking with God today, and not starting to place confidence in years of sobriety from alcohol. That's dangerous.

But there are three more things I want to point out about the penny:

1. You will find the phrase "In God we trust" across the top. Amen. We will be victorious over our struggle by trusting in God; it's in Him that we trust.
2. The word *Liberty* is on the front. How incredible. It is for freedom that Christ has set you free.
3. Abraham Lincoln, the emancipator of the slaves, is pictured. We, too, have an emancipator, as we were once slaves to sin and Satan—Jesus, the one who sets the slaves free.

So find a penny and stick it in your pocket as a reminder that this journey is one day at a time. It's in God that we trust, not our own strength, attempts, or righteousness. He offered His life to give us freedom. And He is risen victorious over sin, death, and Satan, as the one who set the slaves free.

This transformational truth is found in Galatians 5:1.

> For freedom Christ has set us free; stand firm therefore, and do not submit again to a yoke of slavery.

Write a prayer below thanking God for the freedom Christ has for you and that today, by His strength, you will walk in that freedom.

_____

_____

_____

In a position of humility, pray and ask God to keep you from your struggle for the next 24 hours.

Text or call a brother or sister in Christ to let them know if you've stayed free from your struggle for the *past* 24 hours. Tell them you're also committing, by God's strength, to staying free from your struggle/addiction for the *next* 24 hours and you'll follow up with them tomorrow to let them know if you did.

Once you have done so, initial here: ____ Date: _____

>> **SCRIPTURE READING: Galatians 5**

DAY 3

Cash the Check

Praying in faith comes from an abiding faith in the Person prayed to—the confidence is in Him. It is based on a knowledge of who He is, and on a trusted conviction that He is worthy to be trusted. Praying in faith is the act of a simple-hearted child of God.

Corrie ten Boom

CHECKS ARE FUNNY THINGS. The paper itself isn't worth a penny. But what's written on it can be incredibly valuable. A check is a signed document that orders that a person be paid the amount in full when deposited or cashed. I want to tell you about two checks I've written to two people I love.

After our third baby was born, Tim, a friend who's in construction, did some work on our house to convert the back patio into a playroom. In his crazy gospel generosity, he said if we would pay for the materials, he would give us the labor. I'll never forget his kindness. The project took a few months, and when it was completed, I cut the last check, which wasn't a small amount, at least not to us. As time went by and I monitored our bank account, I always had much more than I thought I would. But I would look and see that my friend hadn't deposited the check yet. After two months, I texted my buddy and said, "Our final check hasn't cleared. Would you let me know if you need another one or could you deposit it soon?" He wrote back, "Found it my bag. Thank you. Much needed, so thank you. Depositing now."

The second check was to a young, single mom who my wife and I really love but hadn't seen in years. I bumped into her while she was waiting tables at a restaurant. I wrote her a check and said, "I'm proud of you for raising that little one. I know being a single mom is so hard. You're a hero to us. This is for you and your baby and whatever you need. It's not a ton, but I hope it helps, and our church can help you more with whatever you need." I gave her that check more than a year ago, and it still hasn't been cashed. Maybe she lost it. Maybe she didn't feel like she needed a handout. Maybe it was the fact that she's juggling a hundred pressing things all by herself with a baby and just lost track of it. I hope I run into her sometime soon so we can try again.

So why the story of two checks? Both people needed the money. And both were holding in their hands the very thing that would bring help and relief. One deposited the check and immediately received what was promised. The other received nothing, though she held in her hands the very thing she needed.

If you own a Bible, you hold in your hands a series of checks made out to you as a Christian, signed by God Himself. But like one of my two friends, you must personally believe that the promise is for you and receive it. Believe and receive. This is called *appropriation of a promise*: to personally claim or lay hold of in faith what God has promised for His children. This does not mean you get to claim every Old Testament promise to Israel—those are not for you. But in the New Testament (and even in some of the Old), there are promises, BIG PROMISES, for His children. For you. But you must cash the check, so to say. This book is full of ninety promises for you to personally appropriate, to live in, to believe and receive. So start cashing God's checks. And P.S., they aren't financial; even better, they're eternal.

This transformational truth is found in Romans 4:20–22.

> No unbelief made him waver concerning the promise of God, but he grew strong in his faith as he gave glory to God, fully convinced that God was able to do what he had promised. That is why his faith was "counted to him as righteousness."

Write your prayer below telling God that you believe in Him and His promises for you and that you are fully convinced God will come through on what He promises for His children.

_____

_____

_____

_____

_____

In a position of humility, pray and ask God to keep you from your struggle for the next 24 hours.

Text or call a brother or sister in Christ to let them know if you've stayed free from your struggle for the *past* 24 hours. Tell them you're also committing, by God's strength, to staying free from your struggle/addiction for the *next* 24 hours and you'll follow up with them tomorrow to let them know if you did.

Once you have done so, initial here: ____ Date: _____

>> **SCRIPTURE READING: Romans 4**

DAY 4

A Vital Decision

All is of God; the only thing of my very own which I can contribute to my own redemption is the sin from which I need to be redeemed.

William Temple

WHEN AN EMT ARRIVES at the scene of an accident, they always check one thing first: vitals. They must ascertain before rendering aid whether the person is dead or alive, despite all the other presenting injuries. It doesn't matter if the person's leg has a compound fracture. It doesn't matter how much blood there is. What good would it be to set and splint a broken leg on a dead person? Or try to stop the bleeding of a person who's already passed? Conversely, how unproductive would it be to start giving chest compressions and mouth-to-mouth to a person who's alive, when what they need is someone to stop the bleeding. Thus, the EMT always checks for vitals first.

So it is with us. From the beginning of this journey, you must know whether you are, spiritually speaking, alive (born again) or dead (in sin). If you're born again, what you need is sanctification (to be made more like Jesus by the power of the Spirit, having already trusted in Christ). If you're dead in your sins, you first need justification (to be made right with God by the power of the Spirit through faith in Jesus Christ for the forgiveness of your sins) and *then* sanctification. Born again or dead in sin. That is the question *you* must answer at the outset.

So, if you were to die right now, how certain are you on a scale of 1 to 10 (10 being absolutely certain) that you would go to heaven? Write your answer here: _____

And if you did die and were standing before God and He asked you, "Why should I let you into My heaven?" What would be your answer? Write down your answer here:

_____

_____

_____

_____

If your answer was anything other than *Jesus*, I would offer that you are confused about how we are saved *or* may be placing your hope in good works, being a "good person," the idea that all people go to heaven if they seek God, or the belief you've sinned so greatly you can't be forgiven.

This transformational truth is from Romans 6:23.

For the wages of sin is death, but the free gift of God is eternal life in Christ Jesus our Lord.

What we deserve for our sin is death in this life and hell forever in the next. So God sent Jesus, who is both fully God and fully man, to die for our sins and be raised from the dead. Salvation is found in trusting Jesus for the forgiveness of your sins. There is no other way.

If you are saved, write a prayer thanking God that you are saved and you are His. If you answered less than 10 and/or didn't write *Jesus, grace by faith*, etc., then write a prayer confessing that you are a sinner in need of a Savior. Include that today you place your faith in Jesus for the forgiveness of your sins, believing that He is Lord and that God raised Him from the dead. Pray and give Jesus your life, asking Him to send the Holy Spirit to seal you and live inside of you.

In a position of humility, pray and ask God to keep you from your struggle for the next 24 hours.

Text or call a brother or sister in Christ to let them know if you've stayed free from your struggle for the *past* 24 hours. Tell them you're also committing, by God's strength, to staying free from your struggle/addiction for the *next* 24 hours and you'll follow up with them tomorrow to let them know if you did.

Once you have done so, initial here: ____ Date: _____

If you prayed to place your faith in Jesus today, the Bible says you are a new creation in Christ, you have crossed over from death to life, the Holy Spirit now indwells you and has gifted you for the building up of the church, you are an adopted son or daughter of God, and nothing can separate you from the love of the Father.

As next steps, get a Bible and read it daily (or find a free Bible app or online version); become a member of a local Christ-believing, Bible-preaching church; and be baptized and tell other Christians and non-Christians about your decision to follow Jesus.

>> **SCRIPTURE READING: Ephesians 2**

DAY 5

The Power of Presence

He who prays as he ought will endeavour to live as he prays.

John Owen

GUESS HOW MANY TIMES I've looked at porn in front of my wife? Never. I'd have to be out of my mind. Can you imagine the pain, confusion, conflict (colossal understatement), and dysfunction that would bring? So why don't I ever look at porn around my wife? Because she's *there.* She's with me. And when Laura's with me, I have great accountability. I am reminded of who I am and what I have covenanted to her. I am reminded that sin causes pain to me and her, thus it's relatively easy to turn away from harmful things when she's around. It's the power of presence. You should be asking, "Do you look at porn when she's not around?" No. Fact of the matter is, I haven't looked at porn in fifteen years, about the same amount of time as I've been sober from alcohol. But I've been married for only ten years, so how did I stay free from porn the five years before that? Again, it was the power of presence.

I came to firmly believe in the promise of God's omnipresence: He was with me at all times and I was His and my body was a temple of the Holy Spirit. And furthermore, everything I have is His—so my computer, my phone—all His. And to misuse those or my body in His presence would bring exponentially more pain, confusion, conflict (colossal understatement), and dysfunction. But that doesn't always work, right? You can still believe in the omnipresence of God and struggle with sin; we all do, in fact. We all sin knowing *full* well we are in *full* view of a holy God. So how do we keep from repeating this broken, guilt-ridden pattern?

By a promise from God that I cling to in Galatians 5:16:

> But I say, walk by the Spirit, and you will not gratify the desires of the flesh.

This says that if we "walk" with Him, meaning we go through our day with Him on our mind, bringing Him into our every decision and action, He promises we will not do what we don't want to do. I spend time in the Bible and prayer in the morning, kneel and surrender my day to God before getting in the shower, have prayer reminders set in my phone, pray before meetings, sing worship songs in my car, and talk to people about spiritual things. In doing so, I end up walking in the power of His presence, and thus I don't do what I don't want to do.

Write a prayer below asking God to bring this promise to pass in your life today, and tell Him you want to walk with Him.

_____

_____

_____

_____

_____

In a position of humility, pray and ask God to keep you from your struggle for the next 24 hours.

Text or call a brother or sister in Christ to let them know if you've stayed free from your struggle for the *past* 24 hours. Tell them you're also committing, by God's strength, to staying free from your struggle/addiction for the *next* 24 hours and you'll follow up with them tomorrow to let them know if you did.

Once you have done so, initial here: ____ Date: _____

>> SCRIPTURE READING: Galatians 6

DAY 6

Kill the Mosquitos

The Christian must be consumed by the conviction of the infinite beauty of holiness and the infinite damnability of sin.

Thomas Carlyle

MY WIFE AND I HAVE A "HONEY-DO" LIST that we keep on the kitchen counter. It was born out of conflict. She was at home all day raising the kids and would inevitably find things around the house that I needed to do when I got home. I would arrive home from a long day at work and get peppered with news that the sink disposal was blocked, a door lock was broken, her car needed repairing, etc. That led to conflict, so we agreed to create a list that I could attend to. Soon it became a delight to cross things off the list and serve my wife and kids.

One day I got home, and she had written on the list, "Kill the mosquitos." Our kids were covered in welts and scratching incessantly, and she needed space for them to play outside without their being involuntary blood donors. Now, we live in Dallas, Texas. Mosquitos are an inevitable part of life. It's the equivalent of saying "Honey, please remove the sand from the beach." As a loving, gentle husband, I asked her which of these impossible things she'd like me to do first: cure cancer, print the internet, boil the ocean, or kill the mosquitos. She just smirked (I'm actually much funnier than she thinks) and said, "Would you like a number to call?"

So I called the mosquito company, which guaranteed to keep mosquitos out of our yard. Give me a break. They fly, for crying out loud; if we spray our yard, they'll just come over from the neighbors'. But guess what? The company came and the mosquitos were gone. And I mean, gone. They also said they'd come back anytime we saw mosquitos again. A couple of weeks later, I saw a couple, so I sheepishly called and told them. No questions asked, they said, "No problem. We'll send someone out."

We all have those things in our lives that suck the life out of us. Our addictions, our struggles. We hate them, but we also have just kind of grown accustomed to them. They've been there for as long as we can remember, and no matter our efforts, they always come back. In frustration, we just live with the welts and swat at them without any success. But God.

We call on God to do what we can't do. What we don't have the power to do. Sin is a supernatural problem that demands a supernatural answer. The same frustration I felt when my wife asked me to "kill the mosquitos" is the way we feel when we try to get rid of the sin that plagues us. We can't. And God knows this. He's just waiting for us to call on Him. And when we do, He kills sin. And guess what? He has a guarantee too. When the sin comes back, as it tends to do, we just call Him again. And He again kills what we can't. He's not mad about it; He lives to do it. He delights to help you with sin. He's your Father.

This promise from God is found in Romans 8:13:

For if you live according to the flesh you will die, but if by the Spirit you put to death the deeds of the body, you will live.

Write a prayer below asking the Spirit to put to death your struggle and give you life.

_____

_____

_____

In a position of humility, pray and ask God to keep you from your struggle for the next 24 hours.

Text or call a brother or sister in Christ to let them know if you've stayed free from your struggle for the *past* 24 hours. Tell them you're also committing, by God's strength, to staying free from your struggle/addiction for the *next* 24 hours and you'll follow up with them tomorrow to let them know if you did.

Once you have done so, initial here: _____ Date: _____

>> **SCRIPTURE READING: Romans 8**

DAY 7

An Open Garage Door

Every time you make a choice, you are turning the central part of you, the part of you that chooses, into something a little different from what it was before. And, taking your life as a whole, with all your innumerable choices, all your life long you are slowly turning this central thing either into a Heavenly creature or into a hellish creature. . . . Each of us at each moment is progressing to the one state or the other.

C. S. Lewis

ONE MORNING, we woke up to find that our garage door had been open all night. It may sound like a small thing, but I had this sinking feeling and instant panic. I checked to make sure the kids were still asleep in their rooms. That my wife's purse was still where she had left it. Then I checked every room of our house. We had both slept soundly through the night (an anomaly with kids aged four, three, and one), and anyone could have come and gone and done anything without our noticing. It was unsettling to know that our home and family had been completely exposed and open all through the night.

The irony is that this is what we do daily, but we do it consciously and even intentionally. We have garage doors open on our phones and computers. Garage doors open in our minds. Garage doors open in our field of view and what's before our eyes. Garage doors open in where we go. A person given to worry and fear who doesn't pray about every worry and fear is a home left wide open to every intrusive thought. An alcoholic who thinks just one drink is okay or still hangs out with their drinking friends while they're drinking is vulnerable.

Jesus can lock down every angle from which sin can enter. We have to make sure those evil desires have no way to gain entrance into our lives. Put down the garage door of indifference. Lock the doors of temptation. And make no provision for the flesh.

This transformational truth is from God and is found in Romans 13:14.

> But put on the Lord Jesus Christ, and make no provision for the flesh, to gratify its desires.

Write a prayer below confessing areas of life you have left wide open for temptation, sin, and Satan or asking God to reveal them to you.

In a position of humility, pray and ask God to keep you from your struggle for the next 24 hours.

Text or call a brother or sister in Christ to let them know if you've stayed free from your struggle for the *past* 24 hours. Tell them you're also committing, by God's strength, to staying free from your struggle/addiction for the *next* 24 hours and you'll follow up with them tomorrow to let them know if you did.

Once you have done so, initial here: ___ Date: _____

>> SCRIPTURE READING: Romans 13

DAY 8

Music from a Land Mine

Wherever souls are being tried and ripened, in whatever commonplace and homely ways—there God is hewing out the pillars for His temple.

Phillips Brooks

I SPENT THE SUMMER OF 2008 working with alcoholics in South Sudan with the Kuku tribe. The Sudanese from the north had decimated South Sudan, killing the young men, destroying every building, and then leaving land mines in the fields so the people couldn't farm. As a result, many of the survivors turned to lethal moonshine made in roadside stills from ethanol, embalming fluid, and anything they could find to distill that would alter their state and give momentary peace. This "white stuff" was incredibly addictive and would cause blindness within months and eventually death.

I would walk to the moonshine stills, share my story of alcoholism and freedom, tell them why I was in Sudan, and invite them to a recovery meeting. Every day we would gather under a tree, sing, pray, read Scripture, share a victory and a struggle, and then make a proactive commitment by God's strength to stay sober for 24 hours. Dozens came, and dozens were set free from their addictions by Jesus. The whole town was dumbfounded. The most hopeless drunks were now sober, working, returning to their families, attending church, and filled with inexpressible joy. The moonshiners had no category for such an abrupt change, so they made up lies, saying we must be giving their customers strong American pharmaceuticals and money to keep them from returning to alcohol. They had no other explanation for how the town drunks could so suddenly be free from this fatal addiction. The reality was this: they were simply living out the truths in this book by surrendering to Jesus one day at a time, with a simple 24-hour commitment to staying sober by God's strength. Some moonshiners even started attending our group and following Jesus.

We needed a worship leader for our little church of addicts that met under the mango tree in Kajo Keji, and music is the furthest thing from my gifting. Enter Mr. C, an elderly man who survived the war but had been about to die in the spiritual war of addiction. He and his grown son brought a land mine to our recovery meeting. But this land mine had been gutted of its explosives, covered in goatskin, and strung to make a harp. Our worship was led by a thing previously intended for death and destruction.

You are a land-mine harp. Your sin and struggles and addictions were meant for the death of you—planted by Satan and then furthered by your fleshly desires. But God dug you up from death, gutted out all the destruction, and made you into a thing of worship. Your life has been redeemed and is now meant for God's glory.

The apostle Paul was a walking land mine. He hunted, persecuted, and killed Christians. But God made his life into a thing of worship. That's what Jesus lives to do. He'll do so with you if you ask Him.

This transformational truth written by the apostle Paul is found in 1 Timothy 1:12–14.

> I thank him who has given me strength, Christ Jesus our Lord, because he judged me faithful, appointing me to his service, though formerly I was a blasphemer, persecutor, and insolent opponent. But I received mercy because I had acted ignorantly in unbelief, and the grace of our Lord overflowed for me with the faith and love that are in Christ Jesus.

Write a prayer below asking the Spirit to clean out all within you that brings death today and to make you and your life a thing of worship unto God.

In a position of humility, pray and ask God to keep you from your struggle for the next 24 hours.

Text or call a brother or sister in Christ to let them know if you've stayed free from your struggle for the *past* 24 hours. Tell them you're also committing, by God's strength, to staying free from your struggle/addiction for the *next* 24 hours and you'll follow up with them tomorrow to let them know if you did.

Once you have done so, initial here: _____ Date: _____

>> **SCRIPTURE READING: 1 Timothy 1**

DAY 9

Patience for a
Peanut Butter Sandwich

All who call on God in true faith, earnestly from the heart, will certainly be heard, and will receive what they have asked and desired, although not in the hour or in the measure, or the very thing which they ask; yet they will obtain something greater and more glorious than they had dared to ask.

Martin Luther

WHEN MY FIRSTBORN SON was around three years old, he asked me for a peanut butter sandwich. I was, of course, happy to make him one. Being three years old, he had no ability to get all the ingredients and put it together; it was my job to give him what he needed.

52

I got the peanut butter, bread, plate, and knife and went to work. But as I did, my son began howling as if I had betrayed him and completely denied him of the very thing he wanted. I quickly realized what was going on. He saw me get everything out, but then it disappeared beyond his view on the counter above. For all he knew, I was now using the ingredients for myself or something else or taunting him by not giving him what he wanted and had asked for. He would soon realize that I was not ignoring him but actually making him the sandwich. As he ate it, I sat in silence and realized, *I am just like him.*

I often ask God for what I need and even want. And I think that honors Him. He's proclaimed Himself to you and me as our Father. It's good and right to go to Him for everything. But like my son, I often pray and then look up to God in frustration and disbelief. He's got every resource at His fingertips and can do anything He wants. He says He hears me and knows my thoughts and words. What in the world is taking so long? I have a need, He has the means, so what's the issue?!

I've found that God, in His providence and according to His Word, is always at work. He hears us, He knows what we need and even want, and He's putting things together outside of our view. And in our waiting and hunger and questioning of Him, soon His gracious hand extends to ours and blessings come. Our part is to ask with humility, watch and wait with faith, and then give thanks; His part is to meet every need (and He has promised He will). Don't worry, He hasn't forgotten you; He's just making your sandwich.

This transformational truth from God is found in Colossians 4:2.

> Continue steadfastly in prayer, being watchful in it with thanksgiving.

Write a prayer for something you need below, and tell the Lord you trust that He's at work and will come through and deliver on your needs, just as He's promised.

_____

_____

_____

_____

_____

In a position of humility, pray and ask God to keep you from your struggle for the next 24 hours.

Text or call a brother or sister in Christ to let them know if you've stayed free from your struggle for the *past* 24 hours. Tell them you're also committing, by God's strength, to staying free from your struggle/addiction for the *next* 24 hours and you'll follow up with them tomorrow to let them know if you did.

Once you have done so, initial here: ____ Date: _____

≫ SCRIPTURE READING: Colossians 4

DAY 10

A Gift from a Thief

Every wise workman takes his tools away from the work from time to time, that they may be ground and sharpened; so does the only-wise Jehovah take his ministers oftentimes away into darkness and loneliness and trouble, that he may sharpen and prepare them for harder work in his service.

Robert Murray M'Cheyne

WHEN I WAS FOUR MONTHS SOBER, I was asked to go on a mission trip to an island off the coast of South America with the Kanakuk Institute. I figured I probably wouldn't be down that way again and decided that after the island, I'd backpack in Venezuela and see Angel Falls. When I woke up on the second day, I discovered that my bag had been stolen from our room while we slept. No clothes. No passport. No money/wallet. To add insult to injury, I was left with only deodorant and a terrible pair of Crocs. Two pastors told me two completely opposing truths. One said, "Satan is trying to get you down." Check, mission accomplished. The other said, "God is trying to get your attention." This one I wasn't so sure about, but I was listening. It wasn't until about ten years later that I realized how God used that thief to change the trajectory of my whole life.

Because my bag was stolen, I didn't go to Venezuela and instead returned home to Missouri. Because I was home without plans, the Kanakuk Institute asked me to come and help them prepare for the summer. While I was there, I filled out an application to enroll in their yearlong discipleship program, and it had to have been the worst application they'd ever seen. I handed it in and told the director, "It's not pretty, but it's honest." My first week there, I wrote my mission/vision statement for life. Something deep within me knew I would never go back to business; I was going to spend the rest of my life telling people that Jesus is real, you're never too far gone, and He can change everything. I figured if I was going to do this the rest of my life, I should get further equipped, so I enrolled at Dallas Theological Seminary. My third year of seminary, I met my wife while speaking at Pine Cove Camp. She went on to work at Watermark Community Church in the young adult ministry called The Porch. One month before graduation from DTS, I got an offer to be the men's director of recovery at Watermark for re:generation, our biblically based, Christ-centered twelve-step program.

Why do I tell you this? Because if my bag hadn't been stolen, who knows what would have happened. I might be some vagabond relapsed alcoholic in a South American beach town. Satan was trying to get me down, certainly, but moreover, God was getting my attention—my full, lifelong attention. Satan meant to afflict me with pain; God meant to appoint me with purpose. I thank God my bag was stolen. I count it as one of the greatest blessings in my life.

God will take your problems and give them purpose. You may see the purpose right away, or it could take years. You may not see the purpose until you're at Home with Him one day. But know for sure, God will give your problems purpose.

This transformational truth from God is found in Genesis 50:20.

> As for you, you meant evil against me, but God meant it for good, to bring it about that many people should be kept alive, as they are today.

Write a prayer asking the Lord to help you see the purpose in your problems and to trust Him:

_____

_____

_____

_____

_____

In a position of humility, pray and ask God to keep you from your struggle for the next 24 hours.

Text or call a brother or sister in Christ to let them know if you've stayed free from your struggle for the *past* 24 hours. Tell them you're also committing, by God's strength, to staying free from your struggle/addiction for the *next* 24 hours and you'll follow up with them tomorrow to let them know if you did.

Once you have done so, initial here: ____ Date: _____

≫ SCRIPTURE READING: Romans 12

DAY 11

This Home Ain't Home

We are not only to renounce evil, but to *manifest* the truth. . . . We tell this people the world is vain; let our lives *manifest* that it is so. We tell them that our Home is above—that all these things are transitory—does our dwelling look like it? O to live consistent lives!

J. Hudson Taylor

57

I ASKED MY FRIEND JOE, who is a craftsman, to create a sign to hang in our house that simply says, "This Home Ain't Home." The sign is probably a little confusing to our children, who inherently take things very literally. But it's a truth that I need to be reminded of daily. Our home, our comfy beds, my car, my clothes, our pantry, whatever is or isn't in the bank account—it's not actually mine and certainly isn't going to last.

At the age of thirty, I lost everything. At that timestamp, I had in my name a townhouse in Austin, lakefront property, nice cars, and I did whatever I wanted to do. I thought I was so big-time even though I pitifully wasn't (I was overextended and in debt), but then came alcoholism and its fallout. I soon found myself sleeping on a fraternity brother's couch and had two boxes of wrinkled clothes to my name. All I had worked for was liquidated to pay off debt. It was incredibly painful, but even more so, it was freeing, because what I owned had started to own me. By losing everything, I realized that I am not defined by my things. And so increasingly, I still have things, but my things don't have me.

Because of this reality, I had that little sign made as a reminder that I live for another world, not this one. I live for God, for the kingdom. I am a stranger and sojourner here, and thus my roots aren't deep. I'm a servant, and if He says go, we go. And as such, I can joyfully say as does the sign, "This Home Ain't Home."

There's peace in that. Hope. Comfort. Excitement and anticipation. Freedom. When I know this isn't my home, my life doesn't get hijacked by circumstances, people, and things or the lack thereof. But I still struggle, and so I need the reminder, as do you, friend, that this home ain't Home.

This transformational truth from God is found in Hebrews 11:13–16.

These all died in faith, not having received the things promised, but having seen them and greeted them from afar, and having acknowledged that they were strangers and exiles on the earth. For people who speak thus make it clear that they are seeking a homeland. If they had been thinking of that land from which they had gone out, they would have had opportunity to return. But as it is, they desire a better country, that is, a heavenly one. Therefore God is not ashamed to be called their God, for he has prepared for them a city.

Write a prayer below asking the Lord to free your heart to live as though this home ain't Home.

_____

_____

_____

_____

_____

In a position of humility, pray and ask God to keep you from your struggle for the next 24 hours.

Text or call a brother or sister in Christ to let them know if you've stayed free from your struggle for the *past* 24 hours. Tell them you're also committing, by God's strength, to staying free from your struggle/addiction for the *next* 24 hours and you'll follow up with them tomorrow to let them know if you did.

Once you have done so, initial here: ____ Date: _____

>> **SCRIPTURE READING: Hebrews 11**

DAY 12

Get Naked in Public

One great remedy against all manner of temptation, great or small, is to open the heart and lay bare its suggestions, likings, and dislikings before some spiritual adviser; for . . . the first condition which the Evil One makes with a soul, when he wants to entrap it, is silence.

François de Sales

I TRY TO GET AS NAKED as I can as often as I can with my alcoholism. I'll tell anyone and everyone that I'm a recovering alcoholic. The reason why: it benefits me and them. Here's how it works.

I think about drinking from time to time, usually when stress or anger hits. It's my flesh crying out, "You want some peace? You can get peace in a bottle of Scotch really quickly; you won't have to wait for God or resolve any conflict." But when I share with someone that I'm a recovering alcoholic, I get a tangible reminder as I speak it out loud: I can never drink again. That is death to me.

The other thing it does for me is offer extra accountability. One time I got a scathing email from a woman at our church. She called me a fraud for being so publicly bold about being a recovering alcoholic, yet she had seen me having a glass of wine at a wedding reception recently. The reality is, I wasn't even at that wedding reception and certainly didn't have a drink, but the point is that you have great accountability when you tell others about your struggle.

Lastly, and this is what I've experienced most often, when you get naked with your struggle in public, walls come down. People lean in and share their junk that is deep, dark, and dirty. People can relate to your failures much more than they can your successes. As my friend Chad told me early on, vulnerability breeds vulnerability. When you share your weakness, you make it safe for others to share theirs.

I've had innumerable conversations with executives, waitstaff, homeless people, telemarketers, scammers, grocery store clerks, Uber drivers—you name it—about Jesus, because I first told them about my need for Him: my alcoholism. I don't know that I've ever shared the gospel with someone by starting with "I have a seminary degree." But I have weekly shared the gospel with many by starting with "I used to be an alcoholic." Truly, your mess becomes your message. Nobody needs a Savior apart from their sin. And you can't very well talk about your Savior apart from the sin He saved you from. So get naked with your struggles publicly. It will serve you well and empower you to share Christ with others.

This transformational truth from God is found in Acts 19:18–20.

> Also many of those who were now believers came, confessing and divulging their practices. And a number of those who had practiced magic arts brought their books together and burned them in the sight of all. And they counted the value of them and found it came to fifty thousand pieces of silver. So the word of the Lord continued to increase and prevail mightily.

Write a prayer below asking the Lord for boldness to share your weaknesses with others so you can have a reminder, accountability, and opportunities to share Christ's healing.

_____

_____

_____

_____

In a position of humility, pray and ask God to keep you from your struggle for the next 24 hours.

Text or call a brother or sister in Christ to let them know if you've stayed free from your struggle for the *past* 24 hours. Tell them you're also committing, by God's strength, to staying free from your struggle/addiction for the *next* 24 hours and you'll follow up with them tomorrow to let them know if you did.

Once you have done so, initial here: _____ Date: _____

>> **SCRIPTURE READING: Acts 19**

DAY 13

Self-Portrait of Your Own Death

It is that dying of the old man which is the result of his encounter with Christ. As we embark upon discipleship we surrender ourselves to Christ in union with his death—we give over our lives to death. Thus it begins; the cross is not the terrible end to an otherwise god-fearing and happy life, but it meets us at the beginning of our communion with Christ. When Christ calls a man, he bids him come and die.

Dietrich Bonhoeffer

I LOVE ART, but am not really much of an artist. Nevertheless, I have a self-portrait of my own death in my office. I drew myself on a cross being crucified. Sounds pretty dark and twisted, right? Even blasphemous. It's not. It's quite the opposite, in fact. It's a profound theological truth I have to be reminded of. In the sketch, I'm dressed in a suit (representing pride of life or my old attempts to appear successful), and in one nail-pierced hand is a briefcase with money falling from it (representing the desires of the eyes or my grasping at money and material things) and in the other hand is a bottle of booze (representing the desires of the flesh or my fleshly longings for numbing peace and sinful pleasure). You can barely see it, but on the back of the cross you can make out the back of a head and partially see a crown of thorns. It's me being crucified with Christ.

I see it almost every day, as does anyone who comes into my office. It's a powerful reminder that the old me, the old slave to sin and Satan, is DEAD. That person no longer exists. And now, I'm not better; I'm new. The alcoholic is dead and gone, and now in Christ, I've been raised again to walk in newness of life (Rom. 6:1–4).

You must not only know this truth; you must believe that old you is dead and gone. Now you live for Christ and in the freedom He has bought for you and brought you into.

This transformational truth from God is found in Galatians 2:20.

> I have been crucified with Christ. It is no longer I who live, but Christ who lives in me. And the life I now live in the flesh I live by faith in the Son of God, who loved me and gave himself for me.

Write a prayer below thanking God that the old slave to sin is dead and gone and you have been raised to walk in newness of life.

_____

_____

_____

_____

_____

In a position of humility, pray and ask God to keep you from your struggle for the next 24 hours.

Text or call a brother or sister in Christ to let them know if you've stayed free from your struggle for the *past* 24 hours. Tell them you're also committing, by God's strength, to staying free from your struggle/addiction for the *next* 24 hours and you'll follow up with them tomorrow to let them know if you did.

Once you have done so, initial here: ____ Date: _____

>> **SCRIPTURE READING: Galatians 2**

DAY 14

This Slave Says He Is Royalty

A genuine Christian should be a walking mystery because he surely is a walking miracle. Through the leading and the power of the Holy Spirit, the Christian is involved in a daily life and habit that cannot be explained.

A. W. Tozer

I ONCE HEARD A STORY of a slave auction block. The slaves were brought forth to be sold in the public square. They each were dejected and stripped of their dignity from the cruel mistreatment and abuses of their captors and masters. Except one. One stood strong, chest out in pride and head held high. The auctioneer, attempting to display the slaves' strength and obedience to the bidders, commanded them to do various tasks. From fear of the whip, each completed his task. Except one.

The auctioneer grabbed the slave trader by his shirt and growled, "Does that slave not know I have the power to harm him? The power to even kill him?" The slave trader sheepishly and defeatedly said, "No, no, he knows quite well, but countless beatings and threats haven't affected him one bit. We have never once been able to get him to do a single thing for us."

The slave trader continued, "You see, apparently, this man is royalty in his home country. His father is the king. He won't answer to us and seems to altogether reject us as having any authority over him."

You are royalty. You are not a slave to the cruel master, Satan, though right now you live in this world of which he is the prince of the power of the air. He will continue to relentlessly wield his threats and afflictions on you, but you resist him. Resist him, and God promises he will flee from you. Remember, you are royalty, and your Father is the King—never bow, serve, or answer to anyone else.

This transformational truth from God is found in James 4:7.

> Submit yourselves therefore to God. Resist the devil, and he will flee from you.

Write a prayer below asking God to give you the strength to resist the devil's temptations to act according to his will;

that you would believe and have the power to resist him; and that he, according to Scripture, would flee from you.

_____

_____

_____

_____

_____

In a position of humility, pray and ask God to keep you from your struggle for the next 24 hours.

Text or call a brother or sister in Christ to let them know if you've stayed free from your struggle for the *past* 24 hours. Tell them you're also committing, by God's strength, to staying free from your struggle/addiction for the *next* 24 hours and you'll follow up with them tomorrow to let them know if you did.

Once you have done so, initial here: ____ Date: _____

» SCRIPTURE READING: James 4

DAY 15

The Tale of the Watergiver

It will not bother me in the hour of death to reflect that I have been "had for a sucker" by any number of imposters; but it would be a torment to know that one had refused even *one* person in need.

C. S. Lewis

JONATHAN "JP" POKLUDA, lead pastor of Harris Creek Church in Waco, Texas, is my dear friend and a man marked by generosity. After a particular need he met in my family's life, I wrote this story about him and for him, and now the truth and exhortation to do the same is for you.

In a dry, parched land, there lived a couple of fellows. No one had much at all, but at least these two had something. One had a long metal pipe and the other an old metal pail, while no one else had anything at all. But what good is a pail when you live in a dry and parched land? "About as good as a pipe," said the people of the land.

Both men prayed to God, "God, please give me water." And wouldn't you know it? God blessed them both. The man with the pail couldn't believe his eyes. He thanked God and promptly hid the pail under his bed. *What a treasure. It mustn't spill or spoil*, he thought, fancying himself an awfully good steward. Day after day, he kept praying for more, but it never did come.

Now the man with the pipe was in a pickle. For pipes do carry water, but not like pails. Pipes move water to and fro but never keep it in a hollow. So he scratched his head and said, "Best to share it as the good Lord must've willed than for me to try to keep it and then it be spilled." He leaned his pipe toward a neighbor and gave out a holler: "Don't thank me, thank God before you swaller." The man with the pipe thanked God and smiled, seeing his neighbor surprised and blessed for quite a while. But it occurred to him that his work was not done. Because God filled that old pipe once more, and so he did it again. Neighbor after neighbor and day after day was the rest of the story—each drank their fill and God got the glory.

God made us and blesses us to be conduits, not collectors. This world screams to get as much as you can as quickly as you can—and to keep it all. God says we're blessed when we give. He gives to us to provide not only for us but also to bless and provide for others. We, the church, are the very body of Christ. When we give, it is actually God giving to others in need, and it gives us great joy. My mom has been a lifelong example by constantly giving time, love, and gifts to needs that arise around her, and when people say, "No, you shouldn't . . . I can't accept this," she replies, "Don't take away my joy." She lives the words of Jesus in Acts 20:35: "It is more blessed to give than to receive." Giving on behalf of God. What an insane privilege. And guess what? God says, just like in the story above, that when you give, He'll give to you—not so you can be rich or hoard in some prosperity gospel nonsense, but so you'll continue to be rich in good deeds and rewarded eternally in heaven. Thus, we get the saying "You can't outgive God" *if* your giving is motivated by gospel generosity and not greed.

This transformational truth from God is found in 2 Corinthians 9:10–11.

He who supplies seed to the sower and bread for food will supply and multiply your seed for sowing and increase the harvest of your righteousness. You will be enriched in every way to be generous in every way, which through us will produce thanksgiving to God.

Write a prayer below asking God what you have that He would like you to give to someone else (it could be time, prayer, money, something material, or help).

_____

_____

_____

_____

_____

In a position of humility, pray and ask God to keep you from your struggle for the next 24 hours.

Text or call a brother or sister in Christ to let them know if you've stayed free from your struggle for the *past* 24 hours. Tell them you're also committing, by God's strength, to staying free from your struggle/addiction for the *next* 24 hours and you'll follow up with them tomorrow to let them know if you did.

Once you have done so, initial here: _____ Date: _____

≫ SCRIPTURE READING: Proverbs 11

DAY 16

Everyone Is a Slave to Someone

Souls are made sweet not by taking [ill tempers] out, but by putting something in—a great Love, a new Spirit, the Spirit of Christ. Christ, the Spirit of Christ, interpenetrating ours, sweetens, purifies, transforms all. This only can eradicate what is wrong . . . renovate and regenerate and rehabilitate the inner man. Will-power does not change men. Time does not change men. Christ does.

Henry Drummond

EVERYONE IS A SLAVE, whether they know it or not, like it or not. Every. Single. One. It just depends on who they are a slave to: sin/Satan or Jesus. There is no third option. So really, it's kind of a no-brainer: slave to sin and Satan (who wants you devoured and dead) or slave to Jesus (who wants you to live a full, abundant life). I've been a slave to both, and trust me, Christ is better. If you are in Christ, reject, resist, and renounce your old master and walk in glad submission to your new Master. This is my take on Romans 6. The truths in this chapter of the Bible forever changed my life.

SLAVE

You say that I'm a slave.
Yeah, you used to own me,
Tease, puppet, and control
  me.
You promised to spoil me
  rotten,
But seems like rotten's all
  I've gotten.

You had it running through
  my veins.
Always numbing all my
  pains,
But it never would sustain.

But I tried, imbibed,
And relied on the feeling.
Like a junky needing more,

Getting high and then
　　reeling.
Your lies were crafty,
Always sounded brand new.
Even though time and time
　　again,
I swore I was through.

It was like daily amnesia,
And sweet poison was your
　　feature.
Like a caged, abused beast,
Always promising the feast,
You kept me hungry,
Longing for more.
But you never loved me,
I was only your whore.

And so you fed me and
　　misled me,
Just enough to keep me
　　loyal.
Making me think that
Somehow, someday,
Through all my inner toil,
I could be freed from this
　　disaster.
You cruel, addicting master.
Like a mistreated woman
Who knew no other life,
I went back to the jerk
Despite all the strife.

But while you were sleeping,
Another came knocking.
He grabbed me by my life
With all His crazy talking.
He said that "as a slave,

There's only one way out"
And that His way, the only
　　way,
Was not a safe or easy route.
His solution was to die.
My heart pounding through
　　my chest,
I thought He came to rescue,
But His answer was straight
　　death.

Then this man, like a father,
Smiled as He said,
"You'll no longer be a slave
When your master finds you
　　dead."
Then He took me in his arms
And laid me down into the
　　deep.
Spiritually suffocating,
I tried to wrestle,
But He would keep
Holding me under until I
　　gave in.
It was necessary for this slave
　　of sin
To give up my last breath
Until He verified my death.
It was finished.

THEN, His holy breath filled
　　my chest;
Alive and new, the curse had
　　left.
My old master had no power.
It was no longer his hour.
Now, I was free

71

And didn't have to listen;
He still tried calling,
But my mind had new
    mission.
It was all about my KING.
I was rescued and redeemed.

It couldn't happen on my
    own,
Or by following some rules.
It demanded a savior,
Not the counsel of fools.
It required His death,
And mine as well.
But it didn't stop there,
Now I live to tell;
He rose again, and thus, so
    did I.
He made me new,
Never again will I die.

My old master won't quit
And still tempts me with
    thrill,
But now I hate him
Cause I know his intent is to
    kill.
Now, I won't go back
To the patterns of old;

I am a new slave—
    redeemed, I'm sold.
I have a new Master—
One Christ, one Lord.
Now to Him I cry out
When hungry, tired, or
    bored.

You say that I'm a slave?
Indeed, His solely.
But this slave is now free,
And the result will be holy.
My new Master is good,
Loving, and just.
His life leads to peace
If only you'll trust
In His life and death and
    rising again.
He took your place
And nailed all your sin
To the cross and disarmed
    the enemy.
He is the way, truth, and life
    eternally.
From one slave to another,
Won't you "come and see"?
My Jesus breaks chains
And sets the slaves free!

This transformational truth from God is found in Romans
6:20–22.

For when you were slaves of sin, you were free in regard to
righteousness. But what fruit were you getting at that time
from the things of which you are now ashamed? For the end
of those things is death. But now that you have been set free

from sin and have become slaves of God, the fruit you get leads to sanctification and its end, eternal life.

Write a prayer below acknowledging that you are no longer a slave to sin and Satan but that your Master now and forevermore is Jesus Christ your Lord.

_____

_____

_____

_____

_____

In a position of humility, pray and ask God to keep you from your struggle for the next 24 hours.

Text or call a brother or sister in Christ to let them know if you've stayed free from your struggle for the *past* 24 hours. Tell them you're also committing, by God's strength, to staying free from your struggle/addiction for the *next* 24 hours and you'll follow up with them tomorrow to let them know if you did.

Once you have done so, initial here: _____ Date: _____

≫ SCRIPTURE READING: Romans 6

DAY 17

An Elephant on a String

A prison cell, in which one waits, hopes, does various unessential things, and is completely dependent on the fact that the door of freedom has to be opened from the outside, is not a bad picture of Advent.

Dietrich Bonhoeffer

I READ ONCE (and then regrettably verified it on YouTube) that illegal captors train young elephants by placing a ring of spikes around their ankles or hooks into their necks and then chain them to a tree. The elephant quickly learns that if it pulls the slightest bit to escape captivity, it brings severe pain and wounds upon itself. After the elephant learns this painful lesson, the captors can then lead it with a string tied around its shackled ankle. Literally and logically, the elephant could rip free at any second, but it instead lives with a constant, misperceived fear that the slightest resistance will bring unbearable pain. These massive, strong animals could crush their captors with their power, yet fear keeps them subdued.

Satan has done this to us. Especially us addicts (reminder: that's everyone). He has us hooked to a thing, a pattern, a habit, a person. And when we try to get free from it, it's incredibly painful. We learn that leaving it is more painful than staying in its cruel captivity. So we stop trying. We give up on quitting and resolve, *Oh well, guess I'll just struggle with porn or my eating disorder or codependent relationships for the rest of my life; it's simply too painful to try to leave them.*

But Satan's threats are much more bark than bite. The fact is, the power of sin has been broken already. It feels like

74

captivity, but Christ has already set you free. You need simply to run to Jesus daily, and never yield to Satan's tugs at your flesh and mind. The struggle is just a string Satan pulls; the power of death is no longer in his hands. It's a threat, but just a threat. Break free. You are no longer a *small* elephant. The same power that raised Christ from the dead lives in you.

> *Break free! You elephant on a string.*
> *Once chained with Satan's sting,*
> *You were taught to live in fear;*
> *But no barbs are left to tear.*
> *Twine's threats so loudly stated,*
> *Your strength tho' grown, you've waited.*
> *Your new Master bids you: Come,*
> *Pray. Look to Him and run!*

This transformational truth from God is found in Romans 8:11.

If the Spirit of him who raised Jesus from the dead dwells in you, he who raised Christ Jesus from the dead will also give life to your mortal bodies through his Spirit who dwells in you.

Write a prayer below asking God to give you the courage and belief that you have the same power that raised Christ from the dead and to help you run free from your addiction/struggle/sin, never listening to Satan's threats and temptations.

_____

_____

_____

_____

_____

In a position of humility, pray and ask God to keep you from your struggle for the next 24 hours.

Text or call a brother or sister in Christ to let them know if you've stayed free from your struggle for the *past* 24 hours. Tell them you're also committing, by God's strength, to staying free from your struggle/addiction for the *next* 24 hours and you'll follow up with them tomorrow to let them know if you did.

Once you have done so, initial here: ____Date: _____

>> **SCRIPTURE READING: Romans 7**

DAY 18

Chateau Dlo

Use sin . . . as it will use you. Spare it not, for it will not spare you. It is your murderer, and the murderer of the world. Use it therefore as a murderer should be used. Kill it before it kills you; and then, though it kill your bodies, it shall not be able to kill your souls; and though it bring you to the grave, . . . it shall not be able to keep you there.

Richard Baxter

IN 2008, HAITIANS HELD MASS RIOTS because there wasn't enough food for the people of the country. Child mortality rates were through the roof, and childhood malnutrition was epidemic. So some friends and I spent that summer in Haiti starting a malnutrition clinic for kids. It's still running today, with over one thousand kids served and saved (www.canaanchristiancommunity.com).

Much of Haiti doesn't have basic utilities, including gas, water, and electricity. The children's home I stayed at did have a well that was useful only for washing and bathroom needs. I was told on day one not to drink the water from the well. But one afternoon, we ran out of water. It was July in Haiti, and 120 children and 20 adults had no drinkable water. I had been playing soccer with the kids and decided I would drink the well water. How bad could it be? One full Nalgene later, I felt like I had implanted a brick into my stomach, but the feeling passed and I was good.

One of the last chores my friend did that summer was clean out our *chateau dlo*, the huge, black, plastic tank connected to the well that filled the toilets and provided water for showering. This is where I came to believe the day one rule: don't drink the water. Inside the base of the chateau dlo (Kreyòl for "water house" or tank), where the water goes from the tank to the house, was a collection of a dead bird, rotted leaves, and every infectious microscopic thing imaginable. Yep, I had drunk death.

You drink death too. Likely daily. We have been told the dos and don'ts by God. But when the pressures and desires of life hit, we think, *What could it hurt? I can manage it.* And we drink. We drink what we know we shouldn't. And it might cause a little momentary discomfort of shame or remorse, but it passes soon enough. And we do it again. And again. Enter addiction. But the truth of the matter is, what we are drinking is death. The thing we use, abuse, misuse—it's death. And just because we can't see the sin within and just because some sin has a long incubation term doesn't mean it isn't deadly. The prophet Jeremiah spoke to this:

> For my people have committed two evils:
> they have forsaken me,
>   the fountain of living waters,

and hewed out cisterns for themselves,
  broken cisterns that can hold no water. (Jer. 2:13)

Today, choose to drink living water, not death.

This transformational truth from God is found in Romans 6:21.

> But what fruit were you getting at that time from the things of which you are now ashamed? For the end of those things is death.

Write a prayer below asking God to give you the strength to refuse to drink death today with your struggle of _____ and to instead drink the living waters of the Holy Spirit.

_____

_____

_____

_____

In a position of humility, pray and ask God to keep you from your struggle for the next 24 hours.

Text or call a brother or sister in Christ to let them know if you've stayed free from your struggle for the *past* 24 hours. Tell them you're also committing, by God's strength, to staying free from your struggle/addiction for the *next* 24 hours and you'll follow up with them tomorrow to let them know if you did.

Once you have done so, initial here: ____ Date: _____

>> **SCRIPTURE READING: Romans 1**

DAY 19

A Friend in the Fight

It is precisely when every earthly hope has been explored and found wanting, when every possibility of help from earthly sources has been sought and is not forthcoming . . . it's then that Christ's hand reaches out sure and firm. Then Christ's words bring their inexpressible comfort, then his light shines brightest, abolishing the darkness for ever.

Malcolm Muggeridge

I'VE NEVER BEEN IN A FIGHT IN MY LIFE. Which is super fortunate for me, because I've also never been accused of being muscular. One night (before I was sober), I was with friends for an extended weeklong wedding party. I offended another patron at the bar by getting in his way to take a picture of our group. He got right in my face, and I had seen enough movies to know I was about to get pushed, hit, or knifed. Truth be told, I was adrenaline-shaky scared; he was clearly very mad, and I had no idea why and even less idea of how to fight. But to my surprise, he slowly backed away.

I looked around and saw my friends, two of whom are former US Special Forces, there with me. They had my back. They were watching the whole thing, and unbeknownst to me, *he* was the one in danger and I was safe as could be. I had the right friends around, and the fight just walked away from me.

You're in a fight. Every day. You have a real enemy, and he wants you dead. He wants you engrossed in sin, he wants you to forget God, he wants you to lose sight of the help available to you and always there beside you. But you mustn't. Proportionally, there isn't a lot of dialogue with Satan in the

Bible, but when there is, we probably ought to pay attention. It's good to know about your enemy, but it's even better to know how God deals with your/His enemy. You know what the Bible records the Lord as saying? Twice? That when confronted with evil, we don't rebuke Satan. We ask God to. I have no power over Satan, but you better believe Jesus does. So when I sense darkness, temptation, or evil, I say out loud (Satan can't hear your thoughts), "The Lord rebuke you, Satan." And so should you.

This transformational truth from God is found in Zechariah 3:2.

And the LORD said to Satan, "The LORD rebuke you, O Satan!"

And Jude 9:

The Lord rebuke you.

Write a prayer below about a particular sin struggle and then say out loud with faith, "The Lord rebuke you, Satan."

_____

_____

_____

_____

_____

In a position of humility, pray and ask God to keep you from your struggle for the next 24 hours.

Text or call a brother or sister in Christ to let them know if you've stayed free from your struggle for the *past* 24 hours. Tell them you're also committing, by God's strength, to staying free from your struggle/addiction for the *next* 24 hours and you'll follow up with them tomorrow to let them know if you did.

Once you have done so, initial here: _____ Date: _____

>> **SCRIPTURE READING: Jude**

DAY 20

Don't Fight the Undertow

The secret of being made willing lies in a definite giving up of our will. As soon as we put our will on to God's side, He immediately takes possession of it and begins to work in us to will and to do of His good pleasure.

Hannah Whitall Smith

WHEN WE WERE IN OUR EARLY TWENTIES, some friends and I backpacked through Europe for a couple of weeks. When we got to Spain, we went to the Mediterranean in Barcelona. There were plenty of signs and warnings about the undertow, but I stripped down to my shorts and dove in. I'm a pretty good swimmer and wasn't worried about anything; it's a mild sea, and it was a beautiful afternoon. I floated on my back looking out at the vast, endless water. After a couple of minutes, I rolled over to head back to shore. To my shock, I was about three hundred yards out and could no longer see my friends. Then I felt it: I was being pulled out by a current. Instincts kicked in, and I began freestyle swimming as hard as I could for as long as I could, only to find I was fifty yards or more farther out to sea. I looked for a lifeguard and waved my arms, but no one was looking for me. Then God gave me a thought from years past from swim lessons, summer camp, or who knows where: *When you're being pulled by an undercurrent, don't swim against it, swim parallel to the shore.* With my last bit of energy, I began swimming sideways, thinking, *This isn't going to get me back to land, I'm simply swimming into more water.*

But after a couple of minutes, I found I was out of the riptide. *That's because you can't swim against it; you have to swim away from it.* After I made it out of the current, I was exhausted and began a slow swim back to shore.

Every day, our default setting, even as Christians, is the flesh. An inner desire and strong undercurrent pull us toward sin. Paul records in Romans that we do what we don't want to do. This flesh is the deadly, strong undercurrent of sin that pulls us away from the safety of solid ground. And in our instincts, we think we need to try harder to quit doing x, y, and z. But the harder we try, the further into sin we get. Sin is a supernatural force that demands a supernatural rescue. You don't swim against sin; you swim out of it toward life. And unlike me in the Mediterranean, you have a Lifeguard watching over your every move, waiting for you to call to Him. Swim to Him instead of against the impossible current of sin. He alone is stronger.

This promise from God to rescue you is found in Romans 7:24–25 (and 2 Tim. 2:22):

> Wretched man that I am! Who will deliver me from this body of death? Thanks be to God through Jesus Christ our Lord!

Write a prayer below asking God to save you from the undercurrent of sin and the flesh that is pulling you toward your struggle or addiction. Jesus alone will rescue you and deliver you.

In a position of humility, pray and ask God to keep you from your struggle for the next 24 hours.

Text or call a brother or sister in Christ to let them know if you've stayed free from your struggle for the *past* 24 hours. Tell them you're also committing, by God's strength, to staying free from your struggle/addiction for the *next* 24 hours and you'll follow up with them tomorrow to let them know if you did.

Once you have done so, initial here: ____Date: _____

≫ SCRIPTURE READING: Romans 7

DAY 21

Get Off Your Ass

The Lord also did not think that the teaching of his word alone was enough, but he wanted to give us an example of humility when, girded with a towel, he washed the feet of his disciples. Whose feet do you wash? Whom do you care for? To whom do you make yourself inferior and last of all, since you live alone?

St. Basil the Great

BEFORE YOU GET OFFENDED by today's title, consider it's what Jesus Himself instructs us to do (now some of y'all are really offended).

In the story of the good Samaritan in Luke 10, a man gets beaten, robbed, and left for dead on a road known for trouble. Two men pass him by, but a third stops. The two who pass by are the equivalent of a senior pastor and an associate pastor. Then guess who stops? The outcast. The one who isn't allowed in the temple because he isn't considered worthy by the "holy" people of the day.

Jesus says the outcast gets off his ass, literally and figuratively (your Bible probably says beast, animal, or donkey, but let's be honest—will you remember "Get off your donkey" as well as "Get off your ass"? Didn't think so) and pours both oil and wine on the man's wounds and puts him on his donkey. He puts him up in an inn and pays for the keeper to care for him.

What's my point? It's this: sometimes being focused on our issues, our sin, and our addictions becomes a massive time and energy suck on our lives.

What God tells us in His Word is that our lives are to be marked by loving God and loving others, period. So, one of the best ways to focus on your recovery from sin and struggle is to look upward to God and outward to others, instead of perpetually inward on your sin. Find a fellow traveler on this road of life and help them. In doing so, you'll not only go down in God's history book like the Samaritan, but you'll also forget your own troubles.

Martin Luther King Jr. preached, "The first question that the Levite asked was: 'If I stop to help this man, what will happen to me?' But then the good Samaritan came by, and he reversed the question: 'If I do not stop to help this man, what will happen to him?'"[1] And God says if we do good, our lives will become good. It's the law of sowing and reaping. He says that in helping others, He will help us. So, today, get off your ass, forget about yourself and your troubles and your stigmas, and help someone. God will have good coming to you as you're faithful. That's not karma; it's a promise of God.

This promise from God to do good to you as you do good to others is found in Galatians 6:9–10:

> And let us not grow weary of doing good, for in due season we will reap, if we do not give up. So then, as we have opportunity, let us do good to everyone, and especially to those who are of the household of faith.

Write a prayer below asking God to keep you focused on Him and helping others and not hyperfocused on your sin or past.

_____

_____

_____

_____

In a position of humility, pray and ask God to keep you from your struggle for the next 24 hours.

Text or call a brother or sister in Christ to let them know if you've stayed free from your struggle for the *past* 24 hours. Tell them you're also committing, by God's strength, to staying free from your struggle/addiction for the *next* 24 hours and you'll follow up with them tomorrow to let them know if you did.

Once you have done so, initial here: _____ Date: _____

>> **SCRIPTURE READING: Luke 10**

DAY 22

Witness Relocation

The grace which does not make a man better than others is a worthless counterfeit. Christ saves His people not in their sins, but *from* them.

Charles Spurgeon

A BUDDY AND I WERE OUT roaming backcountry roads and came across an old graveyard. We stopped and looked at all the old graves, pre–Civil War through the early 1900s. One grave immediately stood out like a sore thumb. There among the old, decaying gravestones was a pristine, brand-new granite headstone for two people. But here's what was crazy. The birth dates were normal, but the death dates were a few months into the future, as in planned deaths. We. Freaked. Out. We were telling the story to some friends, and a girl said, "You all need to stop talking about that." Her father had a role in local government, and she told us the graves were part of a cover story for a witness relocation program. A man had attempted to murder two people and was sent to prison. He swore that upon his release, he would kill them. So he was going to be told that those two people had died and were buried there. Those gravestones hopefully guaranteed his would-be victims could live free as they assumed new identities.

This is you, if you are in Christ. Satan wanted you dead. He tried to kill you with sin and circumstances. But in Christ, you've been rescued and ransomed. Satan has no more power over you. You've been given a new identity. So when he knocks on your door of life asking for you, your mentality now is, "Oh, I'm so sorry, that person you're looking for is

86

dead. They were crucified with Christ and no longer live." It's spiritual witness relocation; you've been given a new identity. He'll look for the old you who was his slave to sin, but that person is dead. The tombstone reads the death date of when you placed your faith in Jesus. You are free in your identity that is hidden in Christ.

This promise from God that the old you is dead and your life is now hidden with Christ in God is found in Colossians 3:3.

For you have died, and your life is hidden with Christ in God.

Write a prayer below thanking God that Satan's threats are futile now, the old you is dead, and your new life is now hidden with Christ in God.

_____

_____

_____

_____

_____

In a position of humility, pray and ask God to keep you from your struggle for the next 24 hours.

Text or call a brother or sister in Christ to let them know if you've stayed free from your struggle for the *past* 24 hours. Tell them you're also committing, by God's strength, to staying free from your struggle/addiction for the *next* 24 hours and you'll follow up with them tomorrow to let them know if you did.

Once you have done so, initial here: ____Date: _____

≫ SCRIPTURE READING: Colossians 3

DAY 23

The Pain of Poisonous Pleasures

A little sin, like a little pebble in the shoe, will make a traveler to heaven walk very wearily.

Charles Spurgeon

I LOVED HUNTING IN COLLEGE. One fall morning, I was dove hunting on a Texas ranch with friends. The sun was coming up and the birds were flying. I traced a dove's flight but decided not to shoot because it was low and other hunters were in the field. As I watched, it happened. A yellow flash and instant stinging spread all over my body. I dropped my gun to the ground and involuntarily began checking my face and eyes. An older man who wasn't in our hunting party had been aiming at the same bird and shot. I don't know if he got the bird, but he sure got me. Shotgun BBs hit my face, neck, arms, and chest. I was bleeding in multiple places, but he had shot from far away enough that the pellets had just broken the skin.

A couple of weeks went by and all the wounds had healed except one. My nose had been hit and was badly infected (a couple inches off, and I'd likely be blind in one eye). I couldn't even pull a T-shirt over my head without experiencing excruciating pain. So while bored at a fraternity meeting one night, I decided I had to get the infection out. I began squeezing my nose, and to everyone's surprise (especially mine), a lead BB popped out and bounced across the table. Lead embedded in your body isn't a great thing; it's poison. Not to mention, my injury from the pastime I loved could have been much worse had I been closer to the hunter. That tiny .09-inch lead BB had caused crippling pain and consumed my mind.

I tell you this because a little sin will do the same to you, filling you with pain and poison. Yet sadly, we still have a love-hate relationship with sin. The closer we get, the more deadly it is, but we still toy with it. We are injured all too often by the sin we love in our flesh that we know we should hate in the Spirit. Galatians 5:17 says that the Spirit and the flesh are opposed to each other. Although we don't like to admit it, we love sin because of what it gives us—momentary pleasure, power, pride, a brief semblance of control or escape. We think a small amount won't be too destructive or noticed, but that moment quickly fades and what we are left with is an aching, infecting pain from the poisonous pleasure shot by our enemy. Sin poisons us, and its aim is to kill. Thus, we have to kill it (by the Spirit) before it kills us. Reminiscent of my getting shot, we are told in Ephesians 6:16 that Satan shoots flaming arrows at us.

When Israel was giving their affection to sin instead of to God, he offered them a haunting reality and transformational truth.

Your lovers despise you; they want to kill you. (Jer. 4:30 NIV)

Did you catch that? Your lovers (your sin that you give affection and attention to instead of to God) want to kill you. When we sin or give allowance for a sin struggle to remain, we are inviting death, a known killer and poison, into our lives.

Write a prayer below confessing your love-hate relationship with a particular sin and ask God to remove it, even the smallest amount, before it kills you.

In a position of humility, pray and ask God to keep you from your struggle for the next 24 hours.

Text or call a brother or sister in Christ to let them know if you've stayed free from your struggle for the *past* 24 hours. Tell them you're also committing, by God's strength, to staying free from your struggle/addiction for the *next* 24 hours and you'll follow up with them tomorrow to let them know if you did.

Once you have done so, initial here: _____ Date: _____

» SCRIPTURE READING: Romans 5

DAY 24

Lighting a Twelve-Year Fuse

Blessed are those who have realized their own utter helplessness, and who have put their whole trust in God. If people have realized their own utter helplessness, and have put their whole trust in God, there will enter into their lives two things . . . They will become completely *detached from material things*, for they will know that things do not have the power to bring happiness or security; and they will become completely *attached to God*, for they will know that God alone can bring them help, hope and strength. Those who are poor in spirit are men and women who have realized that things mean nothing, and that God means everything.

William Barclay

I USED TO HEAR when I was a kid and teen that "sin leads to death." I believed it for a little while, but I also watched. No one dropped dead because of alcohol, sex, porn, drugs, or partying. In fact, not only did they not die, they seemed to be having quite a bit more fun than I was having. They weren't bad people; they were really likable people. So I began to question this axiom that sin led to death when it clearly didn't. And I began to question why in the world I was following these stupid rules that kept me from fun. And you know what, I got drunk, I smoked weed, I took pills, I had sex, and it was fun. And I didn't die.

Twelve years into my little experiment to disprove that sin leads to death, I had a shotgun to my head. I was losing everything and truly longed for death.

Sin is a peculiar thing, and it can have a really long fuse. The fuse of my sin burned for twelve years before it was ready to go off and lead to death. Relational death? Check. Physical death? Had three doctors tell me if I didn't quit drinking, I'd be dead soon. Spiritual death? I mocked God, thought I was the one responsible for any success in life, and was surrounded by palpable darkness. Mental death? I had gone mad and was a manic insomniac.

I cried out to Jesus. And started walking with Him daily just like you are doing now. And here's the crazy thing—my circumstances were still the same, but once I set my mind on God, He calmed me. I had life and peace. Hopelessness turned to purpose. Depression turned to joy. Addiction became freedom. Pain became forgiveness. Hate turned to love. Futility turned to intentionality. And that is not just my turn of events. It's the very promise of God to anyone who will walk with Him.

This promise of the power of the Spirit is found in Romans 8:6.

For to set the mind on the flesh is death, but to set the mind on the Spirit is life and peace.

Write a prayer below thanking God that no matter what your circumstances, He will give you life and peace as you set your mind on the Spirit.

_____

_____

_____

_____

In a position of humility, pray and ask God to keep you from your struggle for the next 24 hours.

Text or call a brother or sister in Christ to let them know if you've stayed free from your struggle for the *past* 24 hours. Tell them you're also committing, by God's strength, to staying free from your struggle/addiction for the *next* 24 hours and you'll follow up with them tomorrow to let them know if you did.

Once you have done so, initial here: ___ Date: _____

>> SCRIPTURE READING: Romans 2

DAY 25

Your Pain Is Never in Vain

Afflictions make the heart more deep, more experimental, more knowing and profound, and so, more able to hold, to contain, and beat more.

John Bunyan

I HAVE A FRIEND FROM CHURCH who has visible scars on his face, head, and body from severe burns. It's immediately clear something significant happened to him. But what's also clear is that he is gentle, kind, and humble. Who he is and what he does are inseparably related to what happened to him. But I never knew this until I needed him.

When Ramsey Stone was nine months old, he suffered near-deadly burns when he overturned some hot grease that was on the stove. Doctors told his parents his injuries were unsurvivable and handed them organ donation paperwork. After four months in the ICU, Ramsey was released. Though he doesn't remember the accident, he knew as a child he was different and says, "At some point, I stopped asking why this happened to me and started asking, why did I survive?" Because God had other plans. The scars clearly remained, but so did the providential purpose of pain.

Ramsey knew from an early age that he wanted to be a doctor. As he was supported in his helplessness, pain, and frailty, so he also was inspired to offer that same kindness to others. It would become his life purpose. He gets asked, "How could a good God allow bad things like this to happen?" He tells them, "Come and see."

When I was forty, I needed my fourth hernia surgery (thank you, Adam, Eve, and fallen genetics). I got online and was looking up surgeons in the area. I was shocked when I saw my friend Ramsey. I was further shocked to learn he was rated the number one surgeon in his field. I emailed him, we set up an appointment, and he took care of me. He had never mentioned his profession to me. He went by Ramsey and not Dr. Stone. He doesn't care about titles; he cares about helping people. Ramsey's pain was not in vain. The pain was short-term. The scars were lasting. But the resulting lifework would impact generations, including me.

This will be your story too. God will not waste your pain. If you give your pain and circumstances to God, they will be redeemed and used for good. This is a promise of God. He promises that He Himself will comfort you in *all* your afflictions. There is not a single affliction, struggle, problem, or pain that He will not comfort you in. It's a promise He has made to you in His eternal Word.

So go to God in your pain. He *promises* to comfort you. And moreover, He promises that your pain will not be in vain, but that you yourself will become a comforter to all on His behalf. How's that for a lifework?

This promise that the Spirit prays for you is found in 2 Corinthians 1:3–4:

> Blessed be the God and Father of our Lord Jesus Christ, the Father of mercies and God of all comfort, who comforts us in all our affliction, so that we may be able to comfort those who are in any affliction, with the comfort with which we ourselves are comforted by God.

Write a prayer below asking God to comfort you in a specific place of pain because He has promised to do so, then ask Him to make your life purpose to comfort others in affliction. He will redeem your pain.

In a position of humility, pray and ask God to keep you from your struggle for the next 24 hours.

Text or call a brother or sister in Christ to let them know if you've stayed free from your struggle for the *past* 24 hours. Tell them you're also committing, by God's strength, to staying free from your struggle/addiction for the *next* 24 hours and you'll follow up with them tomorrow to let them know if you did.

Once you have done so, initial here: ___ Date: _____

≫ SCRIPTURE READING: 2 Corinthians 1

DAY 26

Raining Prayer

No heart can conceive that treasury of mercies which lies in this one privilege, in having liberty and ability to approach unto God at all times, according to his mind and will.

John Owen

95

UNLESS YOU'RE A FARMER or a meteorologist, rain is probably just a nuisance and an inconvenience. And most people who are praying about rain are actually just praying that it would stop. But not in Haiti.

The summer I was in Haiti, the country was experiencing a drought and it didn't rain for weeks. A drought in Haiti affects a lot. It means no water collection for purifying drinking water and no water for the plants, and it can make you feel like God has turned His back on you. I'll never forget the day in the summer of 2008 that the heavens opened and it poured like I'd never seen before; it inhibited visibility because it was coming down so hard.

The sound of rain on the tin roof of the open-air dining hall was deafening, but what I saw was spiritually deafening. As everyone went running for shelter, there in the rain, someone stood still. Drenched to the bone. It was Pastor Henri, the man with the vision for the children's home who was discipling me (more with his life than his words). He was standing in the middle of the downpour, face to the rain, arms lifted high, shouting praises and thanksgiving to God. I'll never forget it as long as I live—the sight of that fifty-year-old man humbling himself before God, absolutely covered in the rain he had been praying for and surrounded by his tin can–planted seedlings.

Rain and prayer have much in common.

Water evaporates into the atmosphere. It gathers in clouds, and when pressure systems form, it is released back to the ground. There at the ground, it gives life to the earth, only to return back up to the heavens. It's crazy to think about, but this cycle has continued indefinitely since the flood. Evaporation, collection, precipitation, evaporation, and so on.

It is the same with prayer. We pray and pray and pray (evaporation); God hears, considers, and ordains providential, sovereign plans (collection); He rains down wisdom, blessings, provision, love, and peace (precipitation); and then we bask in the outpouring, faces to God, arms raised in praise. It bolsters our faith that when we pray, God moves. And like the evaporation process, He'll filter out the impurities, and you can be sure that whatever comes back down from His sovereign hand is pure and good and living water. So praise in the rain. Petition up pressure systems. God will hear and collect. And then He will open the heavens and bring life.

This cycle of prayer, blessing, and thankfulness is found in 2 Corinthians 1:11:

> You also must help us by prayer, so that many will give thanks on our behalf for the blessing granted us through the prayers of many.

Write a prayer below thanking God for always being there for you and listening to you. Then thank him for his many blessings.

In a position of humility, pray and ask God to keep you from your struggle for the next 24 hours.

Text or call a brother or sister in Christ to let them know if you've stayed free from your struggle for the *past* 24 hours. Tell them you're also committing, by God's strength, to staying free from your struggle/addiction for the *next* 24 hours

and you'll follow up with them tomorrow to let them know if you did.

Once you have done so, initial here: ____ Date: _____

>> **SCRIPTURE READING: 2 Corinthians 2**

DAY 27

My Kids Own Everything

When asked if Christianity is valid, then why is there so much evil in the world, the famous preacher replied, "With so much soap, why are there so many dirty people in the world? Christianity, like soap, must be personally applied if it is to make a difference in our lives."

Billy Graham

MY YOUNG KIDS OWN A HOUSE IN TEXAS, tons of Craigslist furniture (congrats), a life insurance policy, a bunch of size 11 boots, wedding bands, and two old cars.* Truly, everything we have is theirs. It's even declared that way in some legal writing an attorney friend, Jackie, graciously donated to us when we had kids. And guess what? They act like it. Stickers on the wall? Yes. Of course, to Penny (who's five), it's her wall in her home. Hill, our seven-year-old son, believes he has an inherent right to any media device in our home. Judd, who's three, will climb into your lap to eat your food that he wants. To Judd, it's his, end of story.

---

* If Laura and I were to die, it would all be theirs.

Guess what? Legally, they're more right than wrong (though we're striving against entitlement). And God says the same thing. God's kids own every single promise in the New Testament.** Ephesians 1:3 says you have every spiritual blessing in the heavenly realm. God says you have received them (past tense) because He stands outside of time. But not just that, a literal treasure trove of promises is yours in this life, because Christ has died on your behalf and risen again, making you an heir. The Bible says all the promises of God find their Yes in Him. Now, that doesn't mean every promise in the Bible is yours; some are Old Testament promises meant for the nation of Israel. But the ones in the New Testament? YOURS. Yours in Jesus Christ. You are God's child, and through the death and resurrection of Jesus, you have become an heir.

Like my children do in my house, you should go through the house of the New Testament and start living like those promises are yours—say amen to them. *Amen* is a Greek word that means "let it be so." You've said this promise is mine in Christ? Amen, let it be so, as You've said, Lord. And make no mistake, this is not some promise for prosperity; it's a promise for spirituality. The Bible also promises the sufferings of Christ to overflow to you—the richness is not vain riches but a rich relationship with Christ Himself, now and always.

And be sure to thank God. I want my kids to be blessed, but it sure blesses me when they simply and sweetly thank me for the blessings I give. So don't take these for granted by not personally appropriating them (believing the promise and living in the reality), and don't take them for granted by not thanking God for them. They are gifts and graces, not entitlements.

** Second Corinthians 1:20 says so, if you are in Christ.

The promise that all promises are Yes in Christ is found in 2 Corinthians 1:20:

> For all the promises of God find their Yes in him. That is why it is through him that we utter our Amen to God for his glory.

Write a prayer below thanking God that all promises of the New Testament are Yes in Christ, and to every single one of them, say, "AMEN. Lord, let them be so to me as you have said."

In a position of humility, pray and ask God to keep you from your struggle for the next 24 hours.

Text or call a brother or sister in Christ to let them know if you've stayed free from your struggle for the *past* 24 hours. Tell them you're also committing, by God's strength, to staying free from your struggle/addiction for the *next* 24 hours and you'll follow up with them tomorrow to let them know if you did.

Once you have done so, initial here: _____ Date: _____

» SCRIPTURE READING: 2 Corinthians 3

DAY 28

First Be Reconciled

I have had more trouble with myself than with any other man I have ever met.

D. L. Moody

OFTEN OUR CURRENT STRUGGLES are tied to our unresolved pasts. After college I rented an incredible ranch house on 250 rolling acres, just minutes from downtown Austin. Because sin isn't in a place, it's in a person, our problems have a tendency to follow us. It was a great house for parties, so when it was time to move out, I made sure to discreetly leave a window unlocked so I could return whenever I wanted (pretty sure that's trespassing at best, but more likely breaking and entering). During one such night, having broken in while drunk, I smashed a chandelier and left all the broken light bulbs and glass strewn across the floor.

Later in my life at AA, I did an inventory of my past, which included harms I'd done to others. I prayed and asked God to show me anyone I had hurt. The landlord and owner of that ranch house immediately came to mind, but soon thereafter I moved to Missouri with no way to run into her. *Whew.* Except that two years later I was living in Austin again, and God laid on my heart that I had to make things right with her. But I also had the thought, *She doesn't know it was me. I could send her money anonymously. Her husband is a lawyer—will he press charges? I'm on a better path now; this could disrupt everything.* But as my friend Jonathan Pokluda preaches, obedience is not determined by the outcome. So I pulled $250 from an

101

ATM (which was much more money than I could part with, having quit my job and gone into ministry) and went to where she worked. Heart pounding, I walked through the business doors and was greeted by, "JOHN! Oh my goodness, it's so good to see you! How have you been?" I told her that when I lived at her house, I was an alcoholic and I used to break in after I had moved out. And that one night I smashed out the family room chandelier (did I mention it was the house she grew up in?).

Then I reached into my pocket, pulled out the money, and said, "This is just a start, and I'll give you whatever else I owe you for repairs, cleaning, and used utilities from my parties. I don't deserve it, but would you please forgive me?" She shocked me as she pushed the money back and said, "Oh, I don't even remember that. You and your friends were always so great. How's so and so?" Then God shocked me. The landlord said, "You know, I know someone who is struggling with addiction. Could I give them your contact info?" I told her I would be honored, and just like that, God had flipped the script. I walked out of the business and down those same downtown Austin streets where I had been loaded so many times, but this time the weight of the world had been unloaded because I had made long overdue amends. Regardless of the outcome, I had followed Jesus's command and was more free.

Your turn now. Do you need to seek forgiveness from someone you've wronged? How can you seek to right the wrong? Aside from "I love you," "Will you please forgive me?" is the most often said phrase in my family's home. Life is messy, but God has given us a way to clean up the pieces so relationships don't remain broken. And don't worry about the other person's response. You just be concerned with your obedience, because God is sovereign over the rest of the story.

The transformational truth to seek to right wrongs is found in Matthew 5:23–24:

So if you are offering your gift at the altar and there remember that your brother has something against you, leave your gift there before the altar and go. First be reconciled to your brother, and then come and offer your gift.

Write a prayer below asking God to bring to mind anyone you have harmed. Write down their names. Then ask God how He would have you make things right with them (for a couple of years, I had a list of names in the front of my Bible that I was still seeking to reconcile with, and in time, God helped me cross them all off).

_____

_____

_____

_____

_____

In a position of humility, pray and ask God to keep you from your struggle for the next 24 hours.

Text or call a brother or sister in Christ to let them know if you've stayed free from your struggle for the *past* 24 hours. Tell them you're also committing, by God's strength, to staying free from your struggle/addiction for the *next* 24 hours and you'll follow up with them tomorrow to let them know if you did.

Once you have done so, initial here: ____ Date: _____

>> SCRIPTURE READING: Ephesians 4

DAY 29

Burn the Ships

God has promised forgiveness to your repentance, but He has not promised tomorrow to your procrastination.

Augustine

I HAVE A FRIEND, GRIFF, who has an amazing tattoo on his arm of ships on fire in the ocean. At the time of writing this, he is now three years sober. But when we first talked about burning the ships, it had gotten bad, like huffing solvents bad.

I told Griff a story I had heard and will tell you now. Legend says that in 1519, an "explorer" (read also: person responsible for the holocaust of the Aztecs), Hernán Cortés, landed in the Yucatan in the Aztec Empire. Exponentially outnumbered, he did the most unlikely and unthinkable thing, which should have made his troops mutinous but instead filled them with unstoppable courage. He ordered for their ships to be burned and sank them to the floor of the ocean. In doing so, he set ablaze their only option for retreat. History is undisputed on the rest of the story. Cortés's men knew their only option was to advance.

I told Griff this story because I said, "You have to get rid of every single thing that could lead you back into your addiction: cash, clients, cars, whatever. Burn the ships so that you have no option for retreat. The only option now is to advance against the enemy and get victory." One sober year later, he got the tattoo. Three sober years later, and here I am writing about him in this book. All because he burned the ships and advanced in victory by Christ, never retreating.

The Bible instructs us to advance in Christ and put to death—execute—the things that lead us into sin. So do it now. If you wait, you never will. Burn the ships—today. Block his number. Get rid of the pills and tell your doctor you're addicted to the prescription. Delete the dealer's numbers. Cut the wireless connections. Break up from that sinful relationship. Hide the scales and mirrors. Get the TV and computer out of your bedroom. Share your location on your phone with a friend. Do everything it takes to avoid whatever it is that leads you into sin.

Burn the ships and advance boldly so there is no retreat back to that which leads you into sin.

This transformational truth is found in Colossians 3:2–6.

> Set your minds on things that are above, not on things that are on earth. For you have died, and your life is hidden with Christ in God. When Christ who is your life appears, then you also will appear with him in glory.
>
> Put to death therefore what is earthly in you: sexual immorality, impurity, passion, evil desire, and covetousness, which is idolatry. On account of these the wrath of God is coming.

Write a prayer below asking God to bring to mind Christ's victory over sin, the flesh, and Satan. Ask Him what "ships you need to burn" to never retreat into sin.

_____

_____

_____

_____

_____

In a position of humility, pray and ask God to keep you from your struggle for the next 24 hours.

Text or call a brother or sister in Christ to let them know if you've stayed free from your struggle for the *past* 24 hours. Tell them you're also committing, by God's strength, to staying free from your struggle/addiction for the *next* 24 hours and you'll follow up with them tomorrow to let them know if you did.

Once you have done so, initial here: _____ Date: _____

>> **SCRIPTURE READING: Colossians 3**

DAY 30

A Confessional Psalm

Theirs is an endless road, a hopeless maze, who seek for goods before they seek for God.

Bernard of Clairvaux

WHEN I AWAKE, you are there. When I lie down, you are ever beside me. Even in the watches of the night, you never sleep should I need you. My eyes are ever upon you, and you fill my mind, heart, and soul with great things. You are the source of beauty, wonder, awe, and wisdom. There is none like you, and because of this I have given you my heart. You are close by my side, closer than anyone or anything. And because of you, I will never be alone or lack. Loneliness has fled from me as darkness flees with your light to my eyes. Throughout the day you are my constant companion, and I lack no good thing. As fleeting moments pass, my thoughts and gaze go constantly back to you. You alone are above the wife of my youth, my children, and all; you are first and there is no other. You are my helper, my wisdom, my comfort, my joy. I cannot now fathom a life without your presence. *You are my god. You are my phone.*

One morning I was sitting at my kitchen table to spend time with the Lord reading the Bible and praying. But I kept picking up my phone—just to make sure nothing urgent had hit my inbox, return a couple of texts, check our bank balance, read a text, scan the news for any major headlines. And as I picked up my phone once more, I felt like God was saying this to me: I hate your phone. Then I wrote that psalm above as a confession of sin about my phone.

My smartphone has come between me and my relationship with the Lord. I pray less, and I'm distracted more. I fear my phone gets more of my time than God does.

It's a spiritual plague that must be checked. Consider how your phone and devices are impacting your relationship with God and others. You need to determine how to make a change so it stops changing you.

This call to love the Lord above all and with all is found in Matthew 22:37:

> Jesus replied: "'Love the Lord your God with all your heart and with all your soul and with all your mind.'" (NIV)

Write a prayer below asking God to show you how your phone, media, or anything else is coming between you and your relationship with Him and for the wisdom and power to make specific changes.

In a position of humility, pray and ask God to keep you from your struggle for the next 24 hours.

Text or call a brother or sister in Christ to let them know if you've stayed free from your struggle for the *past* 24 hours. Tell them you're also committing, by God's strength, to staying free from your struggle/addiction for the *next* 24 hours and you'll follow up with them tomorrow to let them know if you did.

Once you have done so, initial here: ____ Date: _____

» SCRIPTURE READING: Deuteronomy 6

CONGRATULATIONS! You've made war against sin for thirty consecutive days now. The first month is always the hardest. But you'll find that the more distance you get from sin, the easier it is to resist. This is a promise from God: "Resist the devil, and he will flee from you" (James 4:7). Keep running to God and resisting temptation, sin, and Satan. You are free!

DAY 31

Getting Hammered

Grace . . . is not looking for good men whom it may approve, for it is not grace, but mere justice to approve goodness. But it is looking for condemned, guilty, speechless and helpless men whom it may save through faith, then sanctify and glorify.

C. I. Scofield

MY IN-LAWS are some of the most generous people in the world. The year before my wife and I had our first child, they took us on a trip to Italy. My father-in-law, Rick, and my mother-in-law, Linda Jo, love creating shared memories, so we covered everything—gondola in Venice, the Colosseum, art in Florence, you name it. But the thing that got my attention the most was something I'd never heard a single person talk about.

Michelangelo is the master sculptor. He created *David*, arguably the most famous sculpture in the history of the world. And we saw it. But as we walked toward it, I stopped in the aisle and was transfixed on what was just yards from the masterpiece. *Prisoners*. The *Prisoners* are a group of four *unfinished* sculptures showing men trapped in tons of stone. They appear to be wrestling to get free but have not been one inch closer to freedom since Michelangelo laid down the chisel some five hundred years ago. But there, juxtaposed with unfinished, rough-hewn *Prisoners*, stands *David*, perfectly sculpted and polished.

I stopped and stared at *Prisoners* rather than *David*, because in that moment, the Lord put something on my heart: that was me; I was once a prisoner—wrestling against the impossible tonnage of sin and not one inch closer for all my efforts and attempts at good works.

But not so in Christ. In Christ, God promises that He will not put down the chisel, painful as it may be sometimes. He will continue shaping you into the image of Christ until His masterpiece is complete in you when you see Jesus face-to-face and will be like Him. He is committed to freeing you and finishing what He began in you. So that addiction or struggle, that thing you want to free yourself from, you can't. But He will. Ask Him to chisel it away. Ask Him today. And may the Master shape you as He has promised.

This promise from God to you is found in Philippians 1:6.

> And I am sure of this, that he who began a good work in you will bring it to completion at the day of Jesus Christ.

Write a prayer below asking God to chisel away the addiction or sin struggle in your life and to not stop until you're free, however painful it may be.

In a position of humility, pray and ask God to keep you from your struggle for the next 24 hours.

Text or call a brother or sister in Christ to let them know if you've stayed free from your struggle for the *past* 24 hours. Tell them you're also committing, by God's strength, to staying free from your struggle/addiction for the *next* 24 hours

and you'll follow up with them tomorrow to let them know if you did.

Once you have done so, initial here: ____ Date: _____

>> **SCRIPTURE READING: Philippians 1**

DAY 32

Identity Theft

Millions of hells of sinners cannot come near to exhaust infinite grace.
Samuel Rutherford

I MET MY WIFE, LAURA, during my third year of seminary. I was in Tyler, Texas, speaking at an event at Pine Cove Camp, and when I got home, my friend who I was staying with said, "Come meet the babysitter." I thought I was going to meet the thirteen-year-old neighbor, but I turned the corner and found Laura. We ended up talking for two hours straight, got coffee the next day, and then talked on the phone that night.

As we talked, she asked where I went to church. I told her. She said, "My aunt and uncle go there."

She told me their names, and I couldn't believe it. "I've had Thanksgiving with your aunt and uncle!" I said. The phone went silent. Seconds went by. "Hello? Laura?"

"I can't believe this," she said.

"Believe what? Did I say something wrong?"

"You're the guy."

"What guy?"

"I can't believe this, you're the guy."

"Laura, what guy?"

"My aunt has been trying to set me up with this guy in Dallas. I think it's you."

"No way. I haven't talked to them in a long time, and they've never mentioned a niece."

"Oh my goodness," she said. "I know everything about you. I know your *whole* story."

Now the phone went silent on my end. I knew what she knew about me: I was a recovering alcoholic who drank hard for twelve years and had only a couple of years' sobriety under my belt. I was unemployed, working odd jobs, back in school at thirty-five, and sleeping on a mattress on my friend's floor. *Gulp.*

But she said something I'll never forget: "I know everything about you, but I'm not going anywhere. I like you more because of what God has done in you."

I felt my identity had been stolen from me by what I had done. I thought what I had done was who I was. Laura drove into my heart with tangible grace what God's Word had said all along: you are NOT what you have done. You are Whose you are. You are defined by Christ, not by your choices or the consequences of those decisions.

I know and love recovered drug addicts, registered sex offenders, a former drug dealer and armed robber, a prostitute, an embezzler, a porn actor, countless porn addicts, a raging psychopath brawler, and more. *All* of them are now amazing, godly people who are dear friends. Because they are not what they have done; they are Whose they are. Christ defines them—and He defines you too.

This transformational truth from God is found in 1 Corinthians 6:9–11.

Or do you not know that the unrighteous will not inherit the kingdom of God? Do not be deceived: neither the sexually immoral, nor idolaters, nor adulterers, nor men who practice homosexuality, nor thieves, nor the greedy, nor drunkards, nor revilers, nor swindlers will inherit the kingdom of God. And such were some of you. But you were washed, you were sanctified, you were justified in the name of the Lord Jesus Christ and by the Spirit of our God.

Write a prayer below claiming you are no longer what you have done but rather you are defined by Whose you are.

_____

_____

_____

_____

_____

In a position of humility, pray and ask God to keep you from your struggle for the next 24 hours.

Text or call a brother or sister in Christ to let them know if you've stayed free from your struggle for the *past* 24 hours. Tell them you're also committing, by God's strength, to staying free from your struggle/addiction for the *next* 24 hours and you'll follow up with them tomorrow to let them know if you did.

Once you have done so, initial here: _____ Date: _____

≫ SCRIPTURE READING: 1 Corinthians 6

DAY 33

Your Part + Their Part = God's Part

[Regarding confession of sin, some] flee from this work as being an exposure of themselves, or they put it off from day to day. I presume they are more mindful of modesty than of salvation, like those who contract a disease in the more shameful parts of the body and shun making themselves known to the physicians; and thus they perish along with their own bashfulness.

Tertullian

MY PARENTS LIVE in the Ozark Mountains of Missouri, one of the most beautiful places in America, with rolling hills, rivers, and all four seasons. One day while driving one of those scenic highways, my dad crossed into a deep median, went airborne, flew through oncoming traffic, flipped, and slammed into a bluff. It's by God's grace that he survived. When the car came to a stop, he regained consciousness but couldn't get out of the vehicle. Three people stopped at the scene, expecting to find him dead. Instead, they were able to call for emergency assistance and get him help. When he got to the ER, the doctors didn't lecture my dad; they cared for him.

When you or someone you know confesses sin, you are able to do the same—but supernaturally. You have a cell phone (prayer) to talk to God when you see someone in the incident of sin (self-inflicted as it may be).

The part of the one who sins is to confess. The part of the one who hears the confession is to pray (call for help, not lecture). Then God does His part, which is to heal.

Confession (your part) + prayer (their part) = healing (God's part).

114

Quit hiding your sin and confess it. God will heal you. It's His promise. Walk it out in faith.

The promise from God for fellowship is found in James 5:16.

> Therefore, confess your sins to one another and pray for one another, that you may be healed.

Write a prayer below asking God to give you the courage to confess your sin and for God to supernaturally heal you.

_____

_____

_____

_____

_____

In a position of humility, pray and ask God to keep you from your struggle for the next 24 hours.

Text or call a brother or sister in Christ to let them know if you've stayed free from your struggle for the *past* 24 hours. Tell them you're also committing, by God's strength, to staying free from your struggle/addiction for the *next* 24 hours and you'll follow up with them tomorrow to let them know if you did.

Once you have done so, initial here:_____ Date:_____

≫ SCRIPTURE READING: James 5

DAY 34

General Order #3

The law is for the self-righteous, to humble their pride. The gospel is for the lost, to remove their despair.

Charles Spurgeon

ON JUNE 19 (celebrated now as Juneteenth), 1865, General Gordon Granger arrived in Port Galveston, Texas, to declare two pieces of information that would change the course of history. One you have certainly heard of: the Civil War was over. The other, many have not heard of: General Order #3.

The people of Texas are informed that, in accordance with a proclamation from the Executive of the United States, all slaves are free.[1]

But there was something terribly wrong with this.

Two-and-a-half years earlier, President Abraham Lincoln had issued a presidential proclamation and executive order freeing all 3.5 million slaves in the South. The tragedy is that this Emancipation Proclamation changed the federal legal status of the slaves to be free, but the legality did not change their reality. Certainly the news of Lincoln's order had made its way south but was withheld from the ears and minds of the slaves, and thus they continued under horrible, sinful oppression (1 Tim. 1:10).

The freed slaves had two different responses to the order. Some left immediately with little more than the shirts on their backs. They faced cruel persecution and isolation as they walked out their new freedom in old enemy lands. Freedom didn't mean ease, but they were finally rightfully free.

116

Others stayed. The old slave masters, fearing the loss of their labor force, offered the bait-and-switch of sharecropping. This meant now-freed slaves lived on the same land, working for pennies in order to have provision. So although they were free, they still lived under constant oppression and threat and didn't fully walk in the freedom that was theirs. And frankly, I do the same thing.

Jesus Christ our Lord has written an emancipation proclamation in Romans 6, that whoever has trusted in Him is no longer a slave to sin or Satan. Yet, rather than walking Homeward in the daily freedom that is already ours, we remain in the darkened land of our previous master, Satan. We will die free eternally but not having heard of or appropriated the freedom that Jesus bought for us in the here and now. That is the legality of the gospel: we are free.

May the legality today, and every day, be your reality. Leave your old masters, sin and Satan, and never return to that slave land.

The promise of this freedom in Christ is found in Galatians 5:1.

> For freedom Christ has set us free; stand firm therefore, and do not submit again to a yoke of slavery.

Write a prayer below asking for God to give you the courage to walk in the freedom today that is already yours in Christ and to supernaturally lead you in freedom from sin and Satan.

In a position of humility, pray and ask God to keep you from your struggle for the next 24 hours.

Text or call a brother or sister in Christ to let them know if you've stayed free from your struggle for the *past* 24 hours. Tell them you're also committing, by God's strength, to staying free from your struggle/addiction for the *next* 24 hours and you'll follow up with them tomorrow to let them know if you did.

Once you have done so, initial here: ____ Date: _____

>> **SCRIPTURE READING: Galatians 3**

DAY 35

Yellow Teeth

If anything becomes more fundamental than God to your happiness, meaning in life, and identity, then it is an idol.

Timothy Keller

"YOUR TEETH ARE YELLOW," my five-year-old son remarked as I brushed his teeth. I thought about saying, "Yeah, well you're short." But he would grow, and my teeth would grow more yellow. It was a losing battle.

Gotta love how kids don't have filters. He wasn't being mean. It was a simple observation. He was making a comparison. His teeth were pearly white and hadn't yet been subjected to two decades of black coffee (not to mention my years previously addicted to tobacco). He was making a comparison.

A comparison. Comparison. Com-par-i-son.

Com-pare-is-sin.

It hit me: to compare is sin. (It's crazy that those words are phonetically embedded in the word comparison.)

What he did innocently, I do sinfully all too often. Meetings, sermons, counsel I offer, ideas I have, how I look (yellow teeth, thinning hair, and all), the additional pounds I carry, the twenty-year-old car I drive—I could fill the rest of this book with all the comparisons I make daily. I give comparisons the power to own me, wreck me, exalt me, embolden me, shrink me. It's evil. In fact, psychologists discovered that social media was causing depression and anxiety, but they didn't know why. When they did follow-up studies, they found that "social comparison" was the source of the sadness. Comparing ourselves to others is lethal to our health—socially, mentally, and spiritually.

God has uniquely created each person. He's given us different bodies, minds, families of origin, ethnicities, opportunities, looks, heights, shapes, gifts, amounts of faith, sufferings for Christ. We even have different struggles with sin—from pride to porn, self-righteousness to self-destruction. Everyone is unique from start to finish, and that's an incredible thing of beauty. But our flesh wants to compare us to one another to find our worth or lose our lack of it. If we are to compare ourselves to anyone, may it be to Christ with a pleading of the Holy Spirit, the Sanctifier (1 Pet 1:2), to shape us more and more into His image.

God made you who you are, every part of you that is not sin. And even the sin, once repented from, He redeems and makes part of your story of redemption if you'll let Him. We must live, by His power, to be thankful for who He has made us and, by His power, cease to make comparisons, for truly to compare is sin.

This transformational truth—not worrying about what others think about you or even what you think about yourself but to be content in what God thinks of you—is found in 1 Corinthians 4:3–4.[1]

> But with me it is a very small thing that I should be judged by you or by any human court. In fact, I do not even judge myself. For I am not aware of anything against myself, but I am not thereby acquitted. It is the Lord who judges me.

Write a prayer below asking God to give you the power to live free of making comparisons.

_____

_____

_____

_____

In a position of humility, pray and ask God to keep you from your struggle for the next 24 hours.

Text or call a brother or sister in Christ to let them know if you've stayed free from your struggle for the *past* 24 hours. Tell them you're also committing, by God's strength, to staying free from your struggle/addiction for the *next* 24 hours and you'll follow up with them tomorrow to let them know if you did.

Once you have done so, initial here: _____ Date: _____

>> **SCRIPTURE READING: 1 Corinthians 4**

DAY 36

Your Choice: A Breeze or a Beating

If you were to rise early every morning, as an instance of self-denial, as a method of renouncing indulgence, as a means of redeeming your time, and fitting your spirit for prayer, you would find mighty advantages from it. This method, though it seem such a small circumstance of life, would in all probability be a means of great piety. It would keep it constantly in your head, that softness and idleness were to be avoided, that self-denial was a part of Christianity. It would teach you to exercise power over yourself, and make you able by degrees to renounce other pleasures and tempers that war against the soul.

William Law

I USED TO HAVE A PHRASE when I was drinking: I'd rather have none than one. Meaning, what's the point of one drink, one beer, one glass of wine; if we're gonna drink, let's get after it and get drunk. Addicts are usually all-or-nothing people, and if they do something, whether good or bad, they're usually full-bore, a train without brakes. Unfortunately for me, this has never only been with alcohol. With ice cream, one scoop is disappointing and six scoops is just right. Laura recently said to me, "You know, I think it's just best that we don't keep ice cream in the house." And she's right. Because my ditch is still to binge on comforts and pleasures. The ingredient may change (alcohol to sugar), but the idol is the same. Idols are deadly—and thus must die.

I've learned a simple secret (from a previous executive pastor) that gives me an incredible amount of resistance to the whims, whispers, and waves of temptation that call to me. It's this: 99 percent is a beating and 100 percent is a breeze.

If you allow yourself to do something 1 percent of the time, you have a 99 percent greater chance of falling into that which you're warring against. For example, if I said, "I don't drink unless it's a special occasion," I'm left wondering every day, *Is this a special occasion?* Job promotion, holiday, birthday, vacation, day off, dinner party with old friends, wedding reception, New Year's. Pretty soon, every day, week, and month has its special occasion, and you're no longer struggling. Instead, it's a beating. When I allow myself sweets 1 percent of the time, I'm always allowing myself sweets. But when I make a line in the sand and say "none" before I'm even faced with the choice, the battle is already won.

You wouldn't believe the number of free drinks that I get offered when I'm having dinner at a restaurant. I'm not sure if it's some kind of cosmic setup or spiritual bait or if everyone gets accidental margaritas dropped off at their table, but I've already decided the answer is always no to alcohol, so it's a breeze. When you decide in advance, I do not do _____ 100 percent of the time, the decision is already made—period— and it's a breeze.

So decide today. You are not, by God's power, going to do any amount of your struggle. It's 100 percent off the table. The decision is already made, and even when you're tempted, it'll be a breeze instead of a beating.

This transformational truth about making a decision in advance about what you will or won't do and making no provision for the flesh and its desires is found in Romans 13:14.

> But put on the Lord Jesus Christ, and make no provision for the flesh, to gratify its desires.

Write a prayer below asking God to give you the decisiveness to have zero tolerance for whatever sin has a grip on you, that no matter what or when or where the offering, the answer is always no.

_____

_____

_____

_____

_____

In a position of humility, pray and ask God to keep you from your struggle for the next 24 hours.

Text or call a brother or sister in Christ to let them know if you've stayed free from your struggle for the *past* 24 hours. Tell them you're also committing, by God's strength, to staying free from your struggle/addiction for the *next* 24 hours and you'll follow up with them tomorrow to let them know if you did.

Once you have done so, initial here: _____ Date: _____

≫ SCRIPTURE READING: 1 Corinthians 1

DAY 37

No Pain, All Gain

It is an abuse to confess any kind of sin, mortal or venial, without a will to be delivered from it, since confession was instituted for no other end.

Francis de Sales

DR. CHAPMAN IS AN OLD FRIEND of mine from college, and now we attend the same church. He's no average doctor; he's the personal doctor for a past president. I started getting horrible headaches in my late thirties. He heard me talking about it and offered to help me.

After a very comprehensive head-to-toe physical examination and testing (including a prostate check that would forever change our friendship), he said I have atypical migraines and explained how to keep them at bay: "You need to cut out caffeine and sugar, get eight hours of sleep, and drink a ton of water."

I left his office so thankful to have an answer. I had told him all my symptoms, and then he checked me out and diagnosed my problem. What incredible relief, right? Wrong!

It didn't do any good to see him, because I didn't take his counsel to change. Instead of drinking tons of water, I drank tons of coffee. I still had my half lemonade, half sweet tea every chance I got (I quit alcohol, not Arnold Palmers). I didn't get eight hours of sleep (this I blame shamelessly on my children). And as for water, I showered daily, but that was it for H_2O.

As a result, the migraines still came two to three times a week. He gave me a prescription that would knock them out in the moment, but they still came about every second or third day. I told him my problem but didn't change my life. The migraines persisted. Just telling the doctor of my affliction didn't heal me.

We do this with sin. We confess, but we don't repent. We talk about our chains and then expect change. But it doesn't work that way with headaches or with sin.

We are told to flee sin by turning toward Christ. Just as I was supposed to stop one thing (caffeine) and start another (water), so we must with stopping sin and starting with Christ.

Come out of pain by walking in the light and find all gain in Christ.

This transformational truth about repentance is found in 2 Timothy 2:22.

> So flee youthful passions and pursue righteousness, faith, love, and peace, along with those who call on the Lord from a pure heart.

Write a prayer below asking God to give you the power to repent: to stop sin *by* starting with Christ—one day at a time.

_____

_____

_____

_____

_____

In a position of humility, pray and ask God to keep you from your struggle for the next 24 hours.

Text or call a brother or sister in Christ to let them know if you've stayed free from your struggle for the *past* 24 hours. Tell them you're also committing, by God's strength, to staying free from your struggle/addiction for the *next* 24 hours and you'll follow up with them tomorrow to let them know if you did.

Once you have done so, initial here: ____ Date: _____

≫ SCRIPTURE READING: 2 Timothy 2

DAY 38

Satan's Sinister Strategy

It is the prisoners, and the blind, and the leper, and the possessed, and the hungry, and the tempest-tossed, who are His special care. Therefore, if you are lost and sick and bound, you are just in the place where He can meet you. Blessed are the mourners. They shall be comforted.

Andrew Jukes

RECENTLY, I WAS SITTING with some men in ministry, and we were confessing our struggles to one another and praying. One shared through tears that he had been having suicidal thoughts. This is a leader in a church—with a family. He had no secret sin, and his life wasn't falling apart. But the thoughts were haunting him. So he confessed them. Then another man in the group said, "I've had the same thoughts before." Soon, half the other leaders at the table had shared that they, too, at one time or another had experienced suicidal thoughts—one that he should drive into a bridge on the way home from work; one that, during an argument with his wife, he should just grab his gun and be done with it; and others confessed ways they had thought about ending their lives. After his confession, we reminded our brother that this was not, in fact, his mind; it was his enemy.

Every time you read about suicide and self-harm in the Bible, it is tied directly to the demonic and Satan. King Saul goes to the witch at Endor and the next day commits suicide. The prophets of Baal cut themselves as a blood sacrifice for demons. Satan enters into Judas, who betrays Christ and commits suicide. The Gerasene demoniac of Mark 5 cuts himself with stones and is possessed by a legion of demons. Jesus

126

says of Satan that he is a murderer from the beginning. It's what Satan does to mock God—he gets people to turn on themselves instead of turning to God, who could heal them. He whispers into minds that self-harm will release the inner pain, that suicide will help escape the pain. It sounds like your own voice and logic, but make no mistake—the lies are from Satan and his demons to destroy you. And I can't fathom someone wanting to obey the voice of Satan, certainly not someone reading this book.

In our day and age, there is an epidemic of self-harm (NSSI = nonsuicidal self-injury) and suicide. *Time* magazine reports suicide rates are up 33 percent since 1999,[1] the *Wall Street Journal* reports a 56 percent increase in suicide among teens and youth,[2] and the American Psychological Association reports that almost one in six college students have engaged in self-harm at least once.[3] So even if you aren't considering committing suicide or self-harming, odds are you have been touched by someone who already has, or someone in your life is wrestling with invasive thoughts about one or both—particularly those struggling with addiction or secret sin, and thus shame and hopelessness. Jonathan Pokluda, a dear friend and pastor, says, "Suicide doesn't end the pain when you're dead; it simply transfers the pain to the living."

Reject Satan's lies. Tell a trusted friend today and run to the healing arms of the Lord.

This call to honor God with your body is found in 1 Corinthians 6:19–20.

> Do you not know that your bodies are temples of the Holy Spirit, who is in you, whom you have received from God? You are not your own; you were bought at a price. Therefore honor God with your bodies. (NIV)

Write a prayer below asking God to help you in your struggle today and thanking Him for His gracious power and support.

_____

_____

_____

_____

_____

In a position of humility, pray and ask God to keep you from your struggle for the next 24 hours.

Text or call a brother or sister in Christ to let them know if you've stayed free from your struggle for the *past* 24 hours. Tell them you're also committing, by God's strength, to staying free from your struggle/addiction for the *next* 24 hours and you'll follow up with them tomorrow to let them know if you did.

Once you have done so, initial here: ____ Date: _____

» **SCRIPTURE READING: Psalm 107**

DAY 39

I of the Hurricane

Fallen man is not simply an imperfect creature who needs improvement: he is a rebel who must lay down his arms. Laying down your arms, surrendering, saying you are sorry, realising that you have been on the wrong track and getting ready to start life over again from the ground floor—that is the only way out of our "hole." This process of surrender—this movement full speed astern—is what Christians call repentance.

C. S. Lewis

AS I'VE SAID BEFORE, in the fall of 2005, I went overnight from a nice house in Austin, lake property, luxury cars, and thinking I had the world by the tail to living on a friend's couch with two boxes of wrinkled clothes. I had horrific nightmares and was manic, depressed, an insomniac, paranoid, suicidal, reckless, and drinking myself to death without reservation. Then in a moment of clarity, I remembered a fleeting prayer I had prayed in college: "God, if I ever leave you, destroy everything."

He did. He turned me over to my sin and used it to destroy everything. I was absolutely broken. Words fall short, but I longed for death because of how destroyed my life was.

Then, after hitting step 3 in Alcoholics Anonymous, I surrendered my life and will to Jesus Christ my Lord. I knelt beside the couch I was living on and prayed a simple prayer of a prodigal son returning, covered in shame and rags of over a decade of sin and squandering: "Lord, I've squandered everything You've given me, but what I have left, it's Yours. Have my life, my body, my soul, my mind, my career, where I live, what I do, my money, my car, my computer, my phone, my days, my relationships—it's all Yours." Life snapped into focus, and I realized all of life was to know Him and make Him known.

And in that glad surrender, He moved me into the eye of the hurricane. I was still losing everything, but I had gained what I could never lose. Jesus gave me peace, purpose, hope, and love. And though my circumstances were swirling and crashing, life was all of a sudden still. I was still. Because of Jesus. He is the "I" of the hurricane.

And no matter what your circumstances right now, surrender to Him every single day. He will move you into the eye of your hurricane, where all is still and clear and peaceful, despite the wreckage all around, because He is the I of every hurricane of life. Surrender to Him now.

This transformational truth about repentance is found in Habakkuk 3:16–19.

> I heard and my heart pounded,
>   my lips quivered at the sound;
> decay crept into my bones,
>   and my legs trembled.
> Yet I will wait patiently for the day of calamity
>   to come on the nation invading us.
> Though the fig tree does not bud
>   and there are no grapes on the vines,
> though the olive crop fails
>   and the fields produce no food,
> though there are no sheep in the pen
>   and no cattle in the stalls,
> yet I will rejoice in the LORD,
>   I will be joyful in God my Savior.
> The Sovereign LORD is my strength;
>   he makes my feet like the feet of a deer,
>   he enables me to tread on the heights. (NIV)

Write a prayer below asking Jesus to be the I of your hurricane. He will give you peace.

_____

_____

_____

_____

In a position of humility, pray and ask God to keep you from your struggle for the next 24 hours.

Text or call a brother or sister in Christ to let them know if you've stayed free from your struggle for the *past* 24 hours. Tell them you're also committing, by God's strength, to staying free from your struggle/addiction for the *next* 24 hours and you'll follow up with them tomorrow to let them know if you did.

Once you have done so, initial here: ____ Date: _____

≫ SCRIPTURE READING: Habakkuk 3

DAY 40

Saved to Be Sent

We have the means to evangelize our country; but they are slumbering in the pews of our churches.

John R. W. Stott

ONE OF MY FAVORITE STORIES in the Bible is in Mark 4 when Jesus took the disciples across the sea of Galilee and they encountered a horrible storm while Jesus slept. The disciples cried out, Jesus calmed the storm, and they crossed safely. But that calming of the storm is not why it's my favorite. It's the who on the other side of the storm.

In Mark 5, we learn that the only reason they crossed the sea and almost died in the storm was to meet the Gerasene demoniac, a naked madman. He was chained by the town to the graves. He broke free from them, which would have meant bloodied wrists and ankles, and cut himself with stones. Why? He was indwelt with a legion of demons.

Imagine the disciples, who had to have been thinking, *We almost died for this? For him?* Jesus cast the demons out into the pigs. Why? Because then the town could see the man wasn't evil; it was the demons within him. The pigs rushed down and died, because demons destroy life. The man, clothed and in his right mind, was then seated at the feet of Christ. Then comes the baffling part of the story.

All throughout Christ's ministry, He told everyone to "come and follow me." This man, now yielded to Christ, said, "Let me follow you." And Jesus said no!

What cruelty. What sorrow. And frankly, what relief the disciples must have felt: *Thank goodness crazy graveyard demon-guy isn't getting on the boat with us.* But then Jesus told him why.

"Go home to your friends and tell them how much the Lord has done for you, and how he has had mercy on you" (Mark 5:19). Jesus had saved him to send him.

The disciples and Jesus got back into the boat and left. But one of the disciples must have found him again long after that fateful day. Because we know the man did what Jesus asked of him, as the rest of the story says, "And he went away and began to proclaim in the Decapolis how much Jesus had done for him, and everyone marveled" (Mark 5:20).

Jesus went through the storm, through death, for the one. You are the one. He came through the storm of sin and even died for you. He did so to save you from all the madness and isolation and self-harm of your sin. To save you. And to send you. Go and tell all that Jesus has done for you. Trust me, trust the Bible—all the people will be amazed.

A life changed by Jesus is the greatest, most undeniable, irrefutable apologetic.

This transformational truth about sharing your story and the gospel is found in Mark 5:18–20.

> As Jesus was getting into the boat, the man who had been demon-possessed begged to go with him. Jesus did not let him, but said, "Go home to your own people and tell them how much the Lord has done for you, and how he has had mercy on you." So the man went away and began to tell in the Decapolis how much Jesus had done for him. And all the people were amazed. (NIV)

Write a prayer below thanking Jesus for saving you, and now ask Him to send you.

_____

_____

_____

_____

In a position of humility, pray and ask God to keep you from your struggle for the next 24 hours.

Text or call a brother or sister in Christ to let them know if you've stayed free from your struggle for the *past* 24 hours. Tell them you're also committing, by God's strength, to staying free from your struggle/addiction for the *next* 24 hours and you'll follow up with them tomorrow to let them know if you did.

Once you have done so, initial here: ____ Date: _____

» SCRIPTURE READING: Mark 5

DAY 41

Sold Out or Sell Out

Still, as of old,
Man by himself is priced.
For thirty pieces Judas sold
Himself, not Christ.
Hester H. Cholmondeley

MY WIFE SELLS EVERYTHING in our house: clothes, kitchen items, paintings, anything. I'll come home and things are out on the patio to be picked up by some buyer. I kind of love it, because she's not a pack rat and makes some money. But I kind of hate it, because if things aren't nailed down, they're at risk. She's literally walked through our house and said, "Everything has a price." She's not looking to retire early; she just doesn't want to accumulate junk.

Are you nailed down? Do you have a price? Sadly, we all have a price for which we're willing to sell ourselves. Too much pressure, strife, angst, anxiety and we'll cave. We have a price for which we'll sell out Christ to have a moment of relief, release, relaxation. It may be a high; an outburst of anger; a binge on food, porn, weed, or alcohol; a hookup; flirting; that emotional affair—Satan will offer you a price daily. Will you sell out?

The only way to not sell out Christ is to be sold out to Him and to know that you yourself have been nailed down—the old slave to sin has been nailed to the cross and crucified with Christ. There is no sin worth selling out for.

Judas was willing to sell out Christ for thirty pieces of silver. May it never be said of us that we are willing to sell out Christ for the momentary pleasure and allure of sin. Decide now that you are nailed down and sold out to Christ.

This transformational truth about repentance is found in Matthew 26:14–16.

> Then one of the twelve, whose name was Judas Iscariot, went to the chief priests and said, "What will you give me if I deliver him over to you?" And they paid him thirty pieces of silver. And from that moment he sought an opportunity to betray him.

Write a prayer telling Jesus that no matter what is offered to you today by the world or Satan, you will not sell out, because you are sold out to Him.

_____

_____

_____

_____

In a position of humility, pray and ask God to keep you from your struggle for the next 24 hours.

Text or call a brother or sister in Christ to let them know if you've stayed free from your struggle for the *past* 24 hours. Tell them you're also committing, by God's strength, to staying free from your struggle/addiction for the *next* 24 hours and you'll follow up with them tomorrow to let them know if you did.

Once you have done so, initial here: ____ Date: _____

≫ SCRIPTURE READING: Matthew 26

DAY 42

Evicting Birds

Temptation . . . cannot be sin; and the truth is, it is no more a sin to hear these whispers and suggestions of Satan in our souls than it is for us to hear the swearing or wicked talk of bad men as we pass along the street. The sin only comes, in either case, by our stopping and joining in with them.

Hannah Whitall Smith

MY WIFE, LAURA, struggles with OCD, obsessive-compulsive disorder. Hers manifests in unwanted thought loops she can't shake. The more she tries to reason her way out of them, the tighter they grip and the deeper they spiral. It goes like this: a gross, inappropriate thought goes through her mind. She thinks, *What is wrong with me that I just thought that? What does it mean that I just thought that? Does that mean that I actually could do that or want that?*

She sets her mind to wrestle the thought with reason and only gets a greater beating. The thought loops and OCD can go for days and rob her joy, peace, and presence. Over the years, we've developed some language around the fits of OCD to diminish its power and start exposing it for what it is. One of these is "birds." Martin Luther is believed to have said, "You can't keep the birds from flying over your head, but you can keep them from building a nest."

That is to say, yes, Laura, I, you, and everyone else—we're all bound to have some absolutely horrible, blasphemous, lustful, terrifying thoughts almost every single day. Crazy thoughts are going to fly like birds through your mind; the trick is to shrug them off and not build them a welcome home by feeding them with attention. Some are from the sinful flesh, some are from our minds, and others still are likely attacks and temptations from Satan and demons. And if you seek to reason with temptation or the tempter, you're not likely to land in a good place.

Thus, on Laura's desk sits a little sign that says this: "Don't believe everything you think." I got it for her to help remind her that not everything that flies through her mind is worth believing or giving attention to. But I realized the sign was incomplete. So in permanent marker on the back, I wrote this: "Think everything you believe." And that is how we fight. Scripture tells us this. We don't win by warring with reason or logic; we win with truth. Truth silences lies, temptations, and terrors. Kick the birds to the curb with the powerful truths of God.

This powerful promise for peace is found in Philippians 4:8–9.

> Finally, brothers and sisters, whatever is true, whatever is noble, whatever is right, whatever is pure, whatever is lovely, whatever is admirable—if anything is excellent or praiseworthy—think about such things. Whatever you have learned or received or heard from me, or seen in me—put it into practice. And the God of peace will be with you. (NIV)

Write a prayer below thanking God that when you think about Him, His goodness, and Scripture, He promises to give you peace.

In a position of humility, pray and ask God to keep you from your struggle for the next 24 hours.

Text or call a brother or sister in Christ to let them know if you've stayed free from your struggle for the *past* 24 hours. Tell them you're also committing, by God's strength, to staying free from your struggle/addiction for the *next* 24 hours and you'll follow up with them tomorrow to let them know if you did.

Once you have done so, initial here: ____ Date: _____

>> **SCRIPTURE READING: Philippians 4**

DAY 43

Sinner Who Saints or Saint Who Sins?

There are only two kinds of men: the righteous, who believe themselves sinners; the rest, sinners, who believe themselves righteous.

Blaise Pascal

SOME PRETTY MESSED UP THINGS are part of my past: alcoholism, breaking and entering, making out with a prostitute, strip clubs, porn and masturbation, weed, pills, cutting, suicidal imaginings, and more. But the reason I can write these things down in a book for my mom, dad, in-laws, children, church, and any random person to read is because of a simple but profound truth:

I am not as much a sinner who saints; I am much more a saint who sins.

There's power in identity. Identity and actions are inextricably intertwined. Olympians are disciplined, mail carriers deliver mail, flight attendants care for those who are flying, teachers teach, doctors treat, sinners sin, and saints are holy (meaning set apart solely to God).

The Bible refers to Christians as saints exponentially more often than it calls them sinners. (For example, in 1 Timothy 1:15 and James 4:8 a Christian is possibly being called in present tense a sinner, yet consistently all throughout the Old and New Testaments, those saved by grace through faith are called *saints* or *hagios* in Greek, meaning "holy ones.") Oppositely, it's those far from God and dead in sin who are called sinners. I believe it's much more powerful and important to remind people they are saints who sin than it is to call them sinners. Calling a believer a sinner just reinforces the idea that "Oh well, that's what I do." And as Paul wrote to the Romans in 6:1, should we sin more that grace might abound? May it never be so.

When God looks at you or talks about you, He calls you a saint. Right now, in your struggle, addiction, no matter your past or present, you're a saint.

How can I have the audacity to call you this regardless of what you've done? Because God does. The Corinthian church was a pretty notorious crowd: a guy was sleeping with his stepmom, there was homosexuality, adultery, drunks, slanderers, and more (Paul lists them in 1 Cor. 6:9–11), yet eleven times in 1 and 2 Corinthians Paul addresses anyone in Christ as a saint. Paul one time calls himself a sinner in 1 Timothy 1:12–17, but the great majority of the time, his name for believers is saint and not sinner. Will you still sin this side of eternity? Yes. Does that mean it's your identity? No. Belief determines behavior. Walk by the Spirit today, dear saint, and you will not gratify the desires of the flesh.

This powerful promise that Christians are called saints is found in 2 Corinthians 1:1–2 (and many other verses).

> Paul, an apostle of Christ Jesus by the will of God, and Timothy our brother, To the church of God that is at Corinth, with all the saints who are in the whole of Achaia: Grace to you and peace from God our Father and the Lord Jesus Christ.

Write a prayer below thanking God that because of Jesus you are a saint, a holy one.

_____

_____

_____

_____

_____

In a position of humility, pray and ask God to keep you from your struggle for the next 24 hours.

Text or call a brother or sister in Christ to let them know if you've stayed free from your struggle for the *past* 24 hours. Tell them you're also committing, by God's strength, to staying free from your struggle/addiction for the *next* 24 hours and you'll follow up with them tomorrow to let them know if you did.

Once you have done so, initial here: _____ Date: _____

≫ SCRIPTURE READING: 1 Corinthians 2

DAY 44

Head Stuck in a Bed

It is impossible for that man to despair who remembers that his Helper is omnipotent.

Jeremy Taylor

OUR FIVE-YEAR-OLD SON, Hill, came running into our room yelling, "Judd is stuck! Judd is stuck!" We ran to Penny's room and found Judd, our one-and-a-half-year-old son, stuck with his head between the mattress and the metal bed frame. Sure enough, stuck, just like Hill had said.

Somehow and for some reason, curiosity I'd guess, he'd decided to see if he could fit through the narrow opening. Likely to his momentary satisfaction, he fit. But there was a problem he and the other children soon realized: he could get in, but he couldn't get out. And in his panic of being trapped, he began crying and wrestling to free himself. The other kids couldn't get him out either. The harder they tried, the worse it hurt.

They needed their father.

I pushed the mattress down with all of my weight and simultaneously pulled out our toddler. Needless to say, he hasn't had his head stuck in a bed since. But here's the thing: I wasn't mad at my son for being trapped; I love my son and wanted him to be free.

Sin is like that. We're curious. It seems feasible, even fun. And truth be told, it is. Let's be honest, no one would ever sin if it didn't offer a momentary thrill. The problem is that sin is a trap; we can get in, but we can't get out. That's what

141

leads to so much frustration in the Christian life. People are stuck and wrestle with all *their* might to get free but can't.

Because the only way out of your struggles is through the Savior. You have no power over sin; Jesus has all power. He has conquered sin, death, and Satan. As you find yourself trapped in sin, *the answer isn't to try harder; the answer is to cry out to your Father,* just as my children did. He isn't mad at you. He is waiting, willing, and all-powerful, and He lives and delights to set you free.

This powerful promise for deliverance is found in Psalm 34:17–19.

> The righteous cry out, and the LORD hears them;
>   he delivers them from all their troubles.
> The LORD is close to the brokenhearted
>   and saves those who are crushed in spirit.
>
> The righteous person may have many troubles,
>   but the LORD delivers him from them all. (NIV)

Write a prayer below to your Father; cry out to Him who rescues you every single time.

_____

_____

_____

_____

_____

In a position of humility, pray and ask God to keep you from your struggle for the next 24 hours.

Text or call a brother or sister in Christ to let them know if you've stayed free from your struggle for the *past* 24 hours. Tell them you're also committing, by God's strength, to staying free from your struggle/addiction for the *next* 24 hours and you'll follow up with them tomorrow to let them know if you did.

Once you have done so, initial here: ____ Date: _____

≫ SCRIPTURE READING: Psalm 34

DAY 45

Premium Carpet Pads

A natural heart is offended every day at the preaching of the Cross. . . . The preaching of another's righteousness—that you must have it or perish—many, I have no doubt, are often enraged at this in their hearts. Many, I doubt not, have left this church on account of it, and many more, I doubt not, will follow. All the offence of the Cross is not ceased. But a broken heart cannot be offended. Ministers cannot speak too plainly for a broken heart. A broken heart would sit for ever to hear of the righteousness without works.

Robert Murray M'Cheyne

OUR CARPET IS GROSS. The previous owner of our house had an indoor dog, and we didn't have the money for new carpets, compounded by our three kids ruining the carpet in every way imaginable.

One day I called a carpet company, and a sales rep showed up at the house with all his binders of samples. We flipped through them and arrived at a stain-resistant style that would hide each child's best attempts to soil the carpet. Then he leaned back, sighed, and said, "Okay, now for the important question." I couldn't have guessed what he was about to say. He looked as serious as a heart surgeon and said, "What kind of carpet pad are you going to use?"

I had no clue and frankly couldn't have cared less, so I chose one from the cheap, squishy foam scraps he had.

He said, "Okay, but you're gonna have stains."

"No," I corrected him, "we are *not* going to have stains, because I chose the stain-resistant carpet."

"Doesn't matter," he said. I thought he was just trying to upsell me on some stinking carpet pad that no one will ever see. Then he blew my mind. "Have you ever cleaned your carpet and then had the stain come back?"

"Yes."

"Well, that's because the stain is down in the carpet pad, like a big stained sponge. You can clean the top, but as soon as any pressure is put on it, the stain comes back to the surface. That's why you need a stain-resistant carpet pad too—one that's impervious to liquids. If the stains can't get in, then your carpet can't be stained. It'll get dirty, but the dirt won't get in below the surface, and you can clean it up easily."

I passed on the carpet but will never forget this lesson. This is exactly why we have to have a new heart from the Spirit (Jer. 31:33; Ezek. 36:26). Our old hearts were full of stains like bad carpet padding. We could clean up our outsides with our best attempts at rule-following or good deeds or trying harder, but eventually when the pressure of life hit, the stains would rise back to the surface. Jesus alone can give us a new heart that is impervious to stains. Sure, despite hating it, we still sin on the surface, but now below the surface we are righteous (in right standing with God). Our hearts are forever clean underneath, with our sins washed away as often as we confess them to the Lord. Thank you, Jesus, the unstainable carpet pad of my soul.

This powerful promise for a clean heart is found in Hebrews 10:22.

> Let us draw near to God with a sincere heart and with the full assurance that faith brings, having our hearts sprinkled to cleanse us from a guilty conscience and having our bodies washed with pure water. (NIV)

Write a prayer below thanking God that you have a clean heart because of Jesus, then confess any sin to Him to have Him wash it away.

_____

_____

_____

_____

_____

In a position of humility, pray and ask God to keep you from your struggle for the next 24 hours.

Text or call a brother or sister in Christ to let them know if you've stayed free from your struggle for the *past* 24 hours. Tell them you're also committing, by God's strength, to staying free from your struggle/addiction for the *next* 24 hours and you'll follow up with them tomorrow to let them know if you did.

Once you have done so, initial here: _____ Date: _____

» SCRIPTURE READING: Hebrews 10

DAY 46

Cold Spaghetti Noodles

If we would be strong and vigorous, we must go to God daily and get grace. A man can no more take in a supply of grace for the future than he can eat enough today to last him for the next six months; or take sufficient air into his lungs at once to sustain life for a week to come. We must draw upon God's store of grace from day to day, as we need it.

D. L. Moody

WHILE SPENDING THAT SUMMER in Haiti during the food crisis, I learned a lesson that has served me well in my spiritual life. One morning I showed up to the open-air, cinder-block-and-tin-roof dining hall and on the table for breakfast was a big plain bowl of cold spaghetti noodles. I was so confused and thought, *I'm not eating cold spaghetti noodles for breakfast; that's sick.* Well, about eight hours later, after being on my feet all day serving kids and moms in the malnutrition clinic, I was feeling a bit malnourished myself. I was starving, weak, and regretting turning down the breakfast pasta.

The next day, I showed up at the dining hall and sure enough—cold spaghetti noodles. I grabbed the bowl, served myself, sprinkled some sugar on top, and ate my noodles with thankfulness, knowing it would sustain me. I haven't had cold noodles for breakfast since and am not sure I ever will. But the lesson has stayed with me for over ten years now.

Something doesn't have to be amazing in order to be sustaining.

When I spend time with God in the mornings, reading the Bible and praying, I long for something amazing: to really hear from Him, to find Him speaking through the living

146

and active Word, to feel close to Him in prayer, to be moved to shouting as I sing on my drive in to work. Yet more often than not, it's not that; it's cold spaghetti noodles of spirituality. It's not a sugar rush of emotionally charged spiritualism, but instead it's sustaining, life-giving daily bread. Not daily steak, but daily bread. Also, as Jesus says, it's not weekly bread, monthly bread, or annual bread; it's daily bread He gives. And that's good for me because if He gave me annual bread, in reality He probably wouldn't hear from me much more than once a year. And so even when you don't feel close to the Lord or feel like He hears your prayers or think spending time reading the Bible or even this book actually helps anything, just remember this: you need daily bread, spiritually speaking, and God will give it to you. He will. Jesus said that the Word of God will sanctify you, turning you from sin and toward Christlikeness. Feelings come and go, so focus on daily intake with prayer, the Bible, and worship. It's not about how it tastes; it's about how He sustains.

This powerful promise for strengthening and changing you is found in John 17:17.

Sanctify them in the truth; your word is truth.

Read a chapter in your Bible and then write a prayer below asking God to sustain you with His living, active Word today.

In a position of humility, pray and ask God to keep you from your struggle for the next 24 hours.

Text or call a brother or sister in Christ to let them know if you've stayed free from your struggle for the *past* 24 hours. Tell them you're also committing, by God's strength, to staying free from your struggle/addiction for the *next* 24 hours and you'll follow up with them tomorrow to let them know if you did.

Once you have done so, initial here: ____ Date: _____

>> **SCRIPTURE READING: John 17**

DAY 47

Stay by Dad

Cover, Lord, what has been: govern what shall be. Oh, perfect that which Thou hast begun, that I suffer not shipwreck in the haven.

Theodore Beza

WHEN WE DRIVE SOMEWHERE, unload, and all three kids are on the ground, I say three simple words:

Stay by Dad.

They know why, and they run to my side. The reason for my command and their response: they're tiny, and Texans like their SUVs. My kids are not currently even the height of most vehicle dashboards or windows, so they're not super visible to drivers. If one of them were to lag behind and a truck started backing up, it wouldn't be good. So I demand they stay by Dad because drivers can see me.

I pulled my kids into the alley behind our house because a squirrel had been run over. I showed them the carnage and said, "This will happen to you if you play in the street and get hit by a car." Later in the church parking lot, I said, "Son, stay by Dad or you're going to get hit. Hill, what happens if you get hit?"

"Squished."

"That's right. And then what?"

You could see another family hurrying to get their kids in their car before Hill shared any more graphic narrative. Laura just smiled, waved, and said through her diminishing smile, "Maybe we have this talk once we're inside the car."

The same is true for us. When we stay by Dad, we won't get hit—by sin, that is. Afflictions, temptations, suffering, trials, and testing will still come, but sin won't hit you. Why? Because God promised so.

This powerful promise that God will keep you from sin if you walk with Him is found in Galatians 5:16.

> But I say, walk by the Spirit, and you will not gratify the desires of the flesh.

Consider the ways and times you could walk with God today. Write a prayer below asking God to help you walk with Him all day and therefore not do what you don't want to do.

In a position of humility, pray and ask God to keep you from your struggle for the next 24 hours.

Text or call a brother or sister in Christ to let them know if you've stayed free from your struggle for the *past* 24 hours. Tell them you're also committing, by God's strength, to staying free from your struggle/addiction for the *next* 24 hours and you'll follow up with them tomorrow to let them know if you did.

Once you have done so, initial here: ____ Date: _____

>> **SCRIPTURE READING: Galatians 4**

DAY 48

One Word for Life

Paul had a lovely way of letting his letters break out into song every now and then. . . . One line in a song that comes in Romans 8 has been a great help to me. Way calls the song a "Hymn of triumph to Jesus." This is the line: "How can He [the Father] but, in giving Him [Jesus], lavish on us all things—all?" "Freely give" means to give lavishly. What do I need today? Strength? Peace? Patience? Heavenly joy? Industry? Good temper? Power to help others? Inward contentment? Courage? Whatever it be, my God will lavish it upon me.

Amy Carmichael

ON A RECENT ROAD TRIP, it occurred to me that our youngest son, Judd, only knows one word. This one word communicates volumes and gets him much of what he wants. Thirsty?

One word. Hungry? One word. Frustrated? One word. Hurt? Yep, same word.

The word is *Momma.*

He, in his helpless desperation and total inability, has one essential word in his vocabulary, yet is able to navigate days and nights because he knows Laura loves and lives to help him. Her job in life at this stage is to raise up godly children, so when he cries, "Momma," she's there.

And truth be told, he has other words; it's just that he alone knows what they mean. He points and babbles, and Laura somehow discerns his needs and even his wants.

Sadly, I think I have, know, and use too many words. I have too many God-given talents, abilities, and gifts. I rely on myself far too much and not enough on God. I have much to learn from my son.

All we actually need is one word: *Father.*

Many have been hurt horrifically by their earthly fathers, but the Father, your heavenly Father, will never hurt you. Ever.

Sad? Father. Lonely? Father. Addicted? Father. Hurting? Father. Lacking wisdom? Father.

We all can take a lesson from Judd. He doesn't call out for things; he calls out for a person who knows his needs and wants. Let's go to God like this—in humility, dependency, trust, and belief that He loves us and lives to care for us. For that is, in fact, what He has promised; after all, He alone is your perfect Father.

This powerful promise that God knows your needs and will meet them is found in Matthew 6:7–8.

> And when you pray, do not heap up empty phrases as the Gentiles do, for they think that they will be heard for their many words. Do not be like them, for your Father knows what you need before you ask him.

Father—the name God has told us to call Him if we are in Christ. In simple, childlike faith and words, write a short prayer below beginning with *Father*, and let Him know your needs.

_____

_____

_____

_____

_____

In a position of humility, pray and ask God to keep you from your struggle for the next 24 hours.

Text or call a brother or sister in Christ to let them know if you've stayed free from your struggle for the *past* 24 hours. Tell them you're also committing, by God's strength, to staying free from your struggle/addiction for the *next* 24 hours and you'll follow up with them tomorrow to let them know if you did.

Once you have done so, initial here: _____ Date: _____

≫ SCRIPTURE READING: Matthew 5

DAY 49

The Ten *C*'s of Seeking God's Will

I fear that many people seek to hear God solely as a device for securing their own safety, comfort and righteousness. For those who busy themselves to know the will of God, however, it is still true that "those who want to save their life will lose it." My extreme preoccupation with knowing God's will for me may only indicate, contrary to what is often thought, that I am overconcerned with myself, not a Christlike interest in the well-being of others or in the glory of God.

Dallas Willard

THE TEN *C*'S aren't some magic formula but instead are some of the biblical ways God reveals His will. I share them with you because I remember the feeling of desperation during the first couple of months of my alcoholism recovery. Just keep in mind as you read that we are to be after God's glory, not ours; and His kingdom, not ours; and by His power, not ours. And God gives His children great freedom. Augustine said, "Love God and do as you please." So don't be paralyzed in the seeking of God's will. It is good and right to lay everything before Him, but He may not give a crystal-clear answer of right or left. As you love Him and follow Him, you'll walk closely according to His ways.

When God was bringing me out of alcoholism, I felt like everything, *literally everything*, was changing. He was changing my desires, my motivations, my hopes. Even my sales job became unappealing because I was there only to try to get rich. But the Lord was changing my heart and identity. I even began questioning if the city in which I was living was best for me, given my unhealthy relationships and addictive

153

patterns. I was googling "How to know God's will" and reading articles on it. I had lived so many years for myself and now I was desperate to live for God.

God says that if you lack wisdom, He will give it to you if you ask (James 1:5). He wants to lead you. God knows what is best. The following ten *C*'s will help you seek God's will according to His Word. Try to see your situation through all ten of these principles. If you focus solely on one principle, you may misinterpret God's will. God's direction may become clearer as you filter your situation through all ten. For instance, if you go off conviction only, your personal desires may cloud your decision. But if your conviction lines up with God's Word, the counsel of other Christians, capabilities, etc., you can begin to have greater confidence that you're walking in His will.

Ten *C*'s of Seeking God's Will

1. **Communication** with God—Prayer to know His will (Ps. 139:23–24)
2. **Conviction**—A sense of right and wrong from God that aligns with His Word (1 Cor. 2:12–16)
3. **Counselor**—Jesus said He would send the Holy Spirit, who would be a Counselor to us and lead and speak to us (John 16:13).
4. **Church**—Glad submission to the leaders of your local church (Heb. 13:17)
5. **Community**—Counsel through those committed to helping you grow spiritually, who know and love you and God (Prov. 15:22)
6. **Canon**—God's Word, the Bible (John 17:17; 2 Tim. 3:16; Heb. 4:12)
7. **Circumstances**—Is this decision even a realistic possibility? Paul felt called to return to Thessalonica, but

circumstances, as organized by Satan, prevented him (1 Thess. 2:8).

8. **Capabilities**—Are you able according to your gifts? For example, you may feel passionate about being a worship leader, but you are unable to carry a note (Rom. 12:3–8; 1 Cor. 12:1–31; Eph. 4:11–13; 1 Pet. 4:10–11).

9. **Cost**—Are you able to do what you are considering doing? The Bible cautions against debt. If you don't have the means to do something, it may be an indication you shouldn't. Conversely, having the means doesn't necessarily mean you should (Rom. 13:8).

10. **Calling**—There seem to be, biblically and experientially, instances in life when certain people sense that God is leading them to do something (Saul in Acts 9, for example).

When I was considering quitting my job and going into a one-year discipleship program, I unknowingly used the steps listed above. I pleaded with God to direct me (1). I felt in my spirit that I was done chasing money to get rich (2). My pastor and his wife thought the discipleship program sounded like a great option (3). Christians close to me thought it was a good idea, though some coworkers and drinking friends thought it was extreme (4). Proverbs 16:16 says, "How much better to get wisdom than gold" (5). I went to some business interviews, but they didn't progress; I applied and interviewed with the discipleship program, and they gave me a full scholarship and a work-study job (6). I eagerly desired to know God's Word and to be discipled. For the first time in over a decade, I had an opportunity to go in a totally different direction (7). People were giving me leadership opportunities (8). I was given a full scholarship for a discipleship program (9) and felt in my soul that there was nothing left for me to do but spend the rest of my life telling others about Jesus (10).

With all of that combined, I made the decision to enter the discipleship program, and it was one of the best decisions of my life. I had peace, joy, and confirmation. It was freeing to trust God and not lean on my own understanding like I had in the past. Though the process of discerning God's will may take some time and wrestling, the result is so good.

God loves you. He wants to help you make both big and small decisions. He has a divine plan for you and has gifted you for a purpose in this plan. Desire to honor God in all you do, as He will make your paths straight. Just remember: all of your life is to know Him and make Him known; the rest is details. Keep that as your boilerplate as you seek His will. And as Jesus prayed, "Not my will, but yours, be done" (Luke 22:42).

This powerful promise that God will lead you is found in Proverbs 3:5–6.

> Trust in the LORD with all your heart,
>   and do not lean on your own understanding.
> In all your ways acknowledge him,
>   and he will make straight your paths.

Write a prayer asking God for His will to be done in your life.

_____

_____

_____

_____

_____

In a position of humility, pray and ask God to keep you from your struggle for the next 24 hours.

Text or call a brother or sister in Christ to let them know if you've stayed free from your struggle for the *past* 24 hours. Tell them you're also committing, by God's strength, to staying free from your struggle/addiction for the *next* 24 hours and you'll follow up with them tomorrow to let them know if you did.

Once you have done so, initial here: ____ Date: _____

>> **SCRIPTURE READING: 2 Timothy 3**

DAY 50

Only the Full Resist the Pull

People do not drift toward holiness. Apart from grace-driven effort, people do not gravitate toward godliness, prayer, obedience to Scripture, faith, and delight in the Lord. We drift toward compromise and call it tolerance; we drift toward disobedience and call it freedom; we drift toward superstition and call it faith. We cherish the indiscipline of lost self-control and call it relaxation; we slouch toward prayerlessness and delude ourselves into thinking we have escaped legalism; we slide toward godlessness and convince ourselves we have been liberated.

D. A. Carson

LAURA GAVE ME eight items to get at the grocery store. Eight. An hour and half later, I had a Walmart cart overflowing and had spent over two hundred dollars. I got home, and she was baffled. "Why did you get all this junk?" she asked. I protested, "Don't worry—I got your eight items." That didn't help, for some strange reason. She was rightly frustrated that I'd come home with sugary cereal, junk food, snack items, and even some toys. I simply pointed to the three kids, like Adam pointing to Eve in the Garden. But the real reason why I got all that junk? I'd shopped hungry.

Life is like that. If I don't get time with the Lord daily, my flesh is alive and well. It hasn't been satiated and subdued by the Spirit and thus is looking for anything and everything to satisfy it. It's unrelenting, and I inevitably end up with much more in the cart of my mind and body than I ever intended for that day. Things like pride, lust, apathy, a critical spirit, eating for sport, bingeing on news, and incessantly checking my email and texts seem to jump off the shelves of life's grocery store. And conversely, when I fill up on the things of this world, I lose my appetite for the things of God, just like my kids not wanting a healthy dinner because they've had sweets or snacks. And still, I look to the Lord and protest, "But I had my quiet time: Bible, prayer, some worship music." Yet at the end of the day, there I am with all that sin in my cart. The lesson I've learned and tell often is this:

Only the full resist the pull.

The only way to resist the pulls of the flesh, the world, and Satan is to be constantly filled up by the Spirit. Quiet times are good, but they aren't sufficient. We are to be constantly drinking in the Spirit, yielding to the Spirit, and seeking to align our hearts and minds to things above. That alone—correction, He alone—has the ability to satisfy our souls. And if we aren't full, we'll succumb to the pull.

Quit trying to battle life's temptations and struggles through habits, life hacks, more effort, and healthy choices. The only antidote for sin is to feast on the things of the Lord.

Then, and only then, will the world's sugary-sweet poisons lose their appeal and reduce their pull.

You've seen this verse before already, but it merits a double reminder. This powerful promise for God keeping you from sin if you walk with Him is found in Galatians 5:16.

> But I say, walk by the Spirit, and you will not gratify the desires of the flesh.

Consider the ways and times you could feast on the things of God today. Write a prayer asking God to help you walk with Him all day and therefore not take in that which leads to death.

_____

_____

_____

_____

_____

In a position of humility, pray and ask God to keep you from your struggle for the next 24 hours.

Text or call a brother or sister in Christ to let them know if you've stayed free from your struggle for the *past* 24 hours. Tell them you're also committing, by God's strength, to staying free from your struggle/addiction for the *next* 24 hours and you'll follow up with them tomorrow to let them know if you did.

Once you have done so, initial here: ____ Date: _____

≫ SCRIPTURE READING: 1 Timothy 6

159

DAY 51

The Only Way Up Is Down

A great many think because they have been filled once, they are going to be full for all time after; but O, my friends, we are leaky vessels, and have to be kept right under the fountain all the time in order to keep full. If we are going to be used by God we have to be very humble. A man that lives close to God will be the humblest of men. I heard a man say that God always chooses the vessel that is close at hand. Let us keep near Him.

D. L. Moody

WHEN MY OLDEST SON WAS FIVE, he was obsessed with natural phenomenons: tsunamis, tornadoes, earthquakes, and especially volcanoes. Despite personally having little interest in them, I strangely now think I know more about volcanoes than the average science teacher. So on a road trip from Texas to Colorado, when we found ourselves driving past Capulin Volcano National Park, I knew we had to stop.

We paid the park fee and began driving the winding road up the dormant volcano. After driving up, we parked our car at the crater and saw the path. Our kids were giddy to hike to the crest, but there was a problem. The path before us clearly led to the top, but it was walled off by a guardrail with signs prohibiting climbing over it. I was so confused, and the kids were growing frustrated. Then I saw it. The entrance to ascend to the top was below us. We had to walk down, past the water station, around a gate, lower still, and then—and only then—could we go ascend the mountain. It hit me.

Like life, you have to go down before you can go up.

Pride is all about being exalted. We want to go up in life and do so quickly. But God, in His kindness, grace, and sovereignty, knows humility is essential and requisite before the heights.

Get low. Make your priority going down before the Lord. Humility is spiritually healthy, and pride is spiritual death. God cares infinitely more about your heart than your height. And beyond that, if you are in pride, you will find God opposing you and your efforts, like that guardrail preventing our ascent. But if you humble yourself before God, letting Him be all, He promises to give you grace, supernatural grace for your life. Grace to help you climb the steep grade, to breathe where the air is thin, to keep you from stumbling.

This powerful promise for God to give you grace when you are humble before Him is found in James 4:6.

> But he gives more grace. Therefore it says, "God opposes the proud but gives grace to the humble."

Confess ways you are living independent from God, making decisions without Him. Then write a prayer below relinquishing your rights and asking God to lead you no matter where the path takes you. Kneel before your King in glad submission and pray.

_____

_____

_____

_____

_____

In a position of humility, pray and ask God to keep you from your struggle for the next 24 hours.

Text or call a brother or sister in Christ to let them know if you've stayed free from your struggle for the *past* 24 hours. Tell them you're also committing, by God's strength, to staying free from your struggle/addiction for the *next* 24 hours and you'll follow up with them tomorrow to let them know if you did.

Once you have done so, initial here: _____ Date: _____

>> **SCRIPTURE READING: James 2**

DAY 52

Lingering Lovers

Study universal holiness of life. Your whole usefulness depends on this. Your sermon . . . lasts but an hour or two—your life preaches all week. . . . If Satan can only make you a covetous minister, or a lover of pleasure, or a lover of praise, or a lover of good eating, he has ruined your ministry for ever. Give yourself to prayer . . . and get your texts, your thoughts, your words, from God.

Robert Murray M'Cheyne

DALLAS IS ONE of the biggest cities in the US, so the odds of running into someone you know is pretty slim. Running into them more than once in the same day, statistically improbable. Yet one weekend in Dallas, I ran into my ex three times. THREE TIMES. How awkward and brutal is that?

All of a sudden, the old memories started flooding in. And have you ever noticed that memories of an ex are always good? I never think about the bad times or the annoyances. So as soon as we crossed paths, my mind started racing back ten-plus years—the fun times, the wild times, the carefree abandon, the laughter, and how it never felt like work but instead like all good all the time. And the more my mind went there, the more I started wondering, *What if that was still my life? That would be more fun than here, juggling three kids, running errands, changing diapers. The same old same old, day in and day out.* I love my wife and kids. So much. But I'm just being honest with my internal dialogue.

Normally it wouldn't be appropriate to use names of exes, especially in a book. But for the sake of authenticity, I'm going to use my ex's name.

Jack Daniels.

You see, I drove by three billboards of Jack Daniels Rye, a new kind of bourbon that didn't exist back when I was still drinking. I looked at those advertisements so longingly, remembering all the good times with Jack Daniels, not the hangovers, regrets, missed days of work, missed decade of my twenties, and crushing addiction. I saw the bottle, the highball glass with glistening ice and that golden, peace-giving liquid, and longed for my ex. But my ex never loved me; in fact, my ex never wanted anything but me addicted and dead. That's sin for you.

You have an ex. And the problem with exes is that they still come around. They seem to find you when you're vulnerable: hungry, angry, lonely, or tired. That's not just a coincidence. Satan will drop your ex right before your eyes or mind at just the wrong moment. Just like my ex, yours probably still kind of lingers around. Even though you have tried breaking up, he or she still calls, still whispers to you, still reminds you of the good times. But you have another love now: Jesus. He is yours and you are His. And an ex has no place in the life of someone in a relationship, especially a covenant relationship with Christ. We cannot have a friendship with an ex because we are now God's.

So you have to be continually leaving your lingering lovers. You have to grow to hate them. You ignore their temptations and run back to the arms of your new love, the lover of your soul.

God is jealous for your love, because you are His, the very bride of Christ, and there is no polygamy with the Lord. All your love rightly must go to Him. Consider who your exes are, and ask God to silence their whispers. Then only give your affection to Him.

This transformational truth that demands we give all our love to God and leave those deadly lingering lovers behind is found in James 4:4–5.

> You adulterous people! Do you not know that friendship with the world is enmity with God? Therefore whoever wishes to be a friend of the world makes himself an enemy of God. Or do you suppose it is to no purpose that the Scripture says, "He yearns jealously over the spirit that he has made to dwell in us"?

Consider the ways God is jealous for your love. Write a prayer below asking God to help you rightly always turn to Him.

In a position of humility, pray and ask God to keep you from your struggle for the next 24 hours.

Text or call a brother or sister in Christ to let them know if you've stayed free from your struggle for the *past* 24 hours. Tell them you're also committing, by God's strength, to staying free from your struggle/addiction for the *next* 24 hours and you'll follow up with them tomorrow to let them know if you did.

Once you have done so, initial here: ____ Date: _____

>> **SCRIPTURE READING: James 3**

DAY 53

Cry to Be Clean

Original sin is in us, like the beard—we are shaved today and look clean, and have a smooth chin; tomorrow our beard has grown again, nor does it cease growing while we remain on earth. In like manner original sin cannot be extirpated from us as long as we exist. Nevertheless, we are bound to resist it to our utmost strength, and to cut it down unceasingly.

Martin Luther

WHEN OUR OLDEST WAS A TODDLER, he was outside playing with the water hose and making mud in the backyard. After he'd had enough and was thoroughly covered in mud, he started toward the back door. But as he ran, he fell on the slippery concrete. He was howling, hurting, and covered in mud. I grabbed him under his arms, trying not to get the mud on my work clothes. And then the gospel happened. Laura came running from inside with total disregard and scooped him up into her arms, covering herself in mud and him in love. I stood there thinking, *My wife and my God are awesome.*

Because that is exactly what God, in Christ, does for us. Every. Single. Time.

No matter how dirty my son was, Laura was gonna hold him, comfort him, and clean him. Their relationship won't ever be broken because of filth. And I would imagine there will be worse things than mud over the course of his life.

When we sin, our relationship with God is *never* broken. God doesn't ask us to clean ourselves up before we come to Him. My son couldn't have cleaned himself up. And neither can we clean ourselves of sin. So God makes a way. He simply asks us to cry out, to confess our mess to Him. Then He, as a loving Father, cleans us and puts away our sin, as far as the east is from the west (Ps. 103:11–12).

Cry out and confess your mess—daily. Fellowship will be unhindered, and He will clean you through the blood of Jesus Christ.

This powerful promise from God about Him forgiving you of your sin and cleansing you from all unrighteousness is found in 1 John 1:9.

> If we confess our sins, he is faithful and just to forgive us our sins and to cleanse us from all unrighteousness.

Write a prayer below confessing your sins to God, and ask Him to clean you of all unrighteousness. He is faithful, meaning He will do it every time. And He's just, meaning He alone can atone for sin through Jesus.

In a position of humility, pray and ask God to keep you from your struggle for the next 24 hours.

Text or call a brother or sister in Christ to let them know if you've stayed free from your struggle for the *past* 24 hours. Tell them you're also committing, by God's strength, to staying free from your struggle/addiction for the *next* 24 hours and you'll follow up with them tomorrow to let them know if you did.

Once you have done so, initial here: _____ Date: _____

>> **SCRIPTURE READING: 1 John 1**

DAY 54

A Dead Dog and a Living God

It is to no purpose to boast of Christ, if we have not an evidence of his graces in our hearts and lives. But unto whom he is the hope of future glory, unto them he is the life of present grace.

John Owen

WE KNOW FROM HISTORY that about three thousand years ago in Israel, there was a boy named Mephibosheth, which is an unfortunate name. Not so much because it's hard to pronounce but because it means "dying one of shame." When Mephibosheth was a little boy, soldiers came to kill his family because they were royalty and he could possibly reign as king when he was older. His grandfather, King Saul, and father, Jonathan, died in battle. In a rush to escape, his nanny dropped him and broke both his legs. Without any medical care, his bones didn't heal well, leaving him crippled in both legs. To make matters worse, he was left without family in a place called Lo Debar, which means "nothing." Dying One of Shame was in a wasteland called Nothing.

In the ancient Near East, when a new king took the throne, people would often kill any remaining family members of the old regime, lest they one day rise up and try to reclaim the throne. When the new king, David, summoned a servant to bring Mephibosheth to Israel, Mephibosheth must have been terrified for his life.

David shouted his name upon seeing him: "Mephibosheth!" And in Hebrew, everyone would have heard "dying one of shame" and feared the worst. But David's next words would alter the rest of Mephibosheth's life: "Do not fear, for I will show you kindness for the sake of your father Jonathan, and I will restore to you all the land of Saul your [grand]father, and you shall eat at my table always" (2 Sam. 9:7).

Mephibosheth was in shock. Scripture records his reply: "And he paid homage and said, 'What is your servant, that you should show regard for a dead dog such as I?'" (v. 8).

Dead dog. A dead dog like me. He was saying, "I am the lowest of the low. Why in the world would you ever care for me or about me? I can offer you nothing. I am crippled. I can't work. I can't fight. My family is no longer royalty."

But David had made a covenant with Mephibosheth's dad, Jonathan, that he would always show kindness to Jonathan's descendants. David upheld his covenant, and it would change the entire course of Mephibosheth's life. Scripture states that Mephibosheth ate at the king's table all his remaining days and concludes by reminding the reader, "He was lame in both his feet" (v. 13). From dying one to dining with the king.

Here's the thing: you are Mephibosheth. And so am I. We were dead dogs, dying ones of shame because of what we had done. Spiritually crippled, we were living in nothingness, souls destitute in a wasteland of sin. We deserved death. We were children of wrath and enemies of God. But God the Father summoned you. He called you. He called you because His Son, Jesus, made a covenant, the New Covenant. And having trusted in Jesus and been washed by His blood, now indwelt by the Holy Spirit, you have been adopted by the Father through the Son (Eph. 1:5). And not only that, but like Mephibosheth, you now eat at the Father's table all your life—which is communion, or the Lord's Supper. You have been reconciled to the Father and adopted into His family. And thus, because of Jesus, you have gone from dog to God. What a Savior.

This powerful promise that you are not identified by your past and have been reconciled to the Father is found in 2 Corinthians 5:17–18.

> Therefore, if anyone is in Christ, he is a new creation. The old has passed away; behold, the new has come. All this is from God, who through Christ reconciled us to himself.

Consider the ways you were a dead dog, dying of shame and spiritually crippled. Now write a prayer below thanking God that He called you and adopted you and you will sit at the King's table forever.

In a position of humility, pray and ask God to keep you from your struggle for the next 24 hours.

Text or call a brother or sister in Christ to let them know if you've stayed free from your struggle for the *past* 24 hours. Tell them you're also committing, by God's strength, to staying free from your struggle/addiction for the *next* 24 hours and you'll follow up with them tomorrow to let them know if you did.

Once you have done so, initial here: _____ Date: _____

>> **SCRIPTURE READING: Ephesians 1**

DAY 55

Highest + Least = Greatest

God does not love us because of who we are and what we have done, but because of who God is. Grace flows to all who accept it. Jesus forgave an adulteress, a thief on the cross, a disciple who had denied ever knowing him. Grace is absolute, all-encompassing. It extends even to people who nailed Jesus to the cross: "Father forgive them, for they do not know what they are doing" were among the last words he spoke on earth.

Philip Yancey

WHEN MY BIG BROTHER, Matt, would go on dates, I'd always ask him afterward how it went. He'd say the craziest things, so it was always entertaining. "Ah, I don't think it's going to work; she chews her food kind of weird." Another date: "She wore these funny tennis shoes—can't do it." Said "like" too much. Tilted her head to one side. Talked about flossing.

Who knows why, but the smallest thing would torpedo every date. He was literally the pickiest dater in the history of history. I often thought, *This guy is never going to get married; he's got the highest standards.*

So for that reason, for the rest of my life, I will never forget the night he called from Dallas, Texas, and told me, "John, I've found the girl I'm going to marry." After years and years of his impossibly high dating standards, I couldn't wait to hear who this embodiment of perfection was. He said, "Her name is Mandy. She has cystic fibrosis, a terminal lung disease, and she lives in California. I don't know if God will give us three years or even one, but it doesn't matter. I'm going to marry her." I couldn't believe my ears. This guy with the highest standards had chosen the least likely person, a girl who might not live to see their third anniversary. When I shared this entry with my brother, he said, "Mandy's disease that she was born with could be deemed 'broken' from a worldly perspective, but the sin I was born with is evidence of my 'brokenness.' If the Lord can love me despite my brokenness (my sin), how could I not pursue the love of my life because she was born with a lung disease?"

Well, they just celebrated their sixteenth anniversary and are living their love story. Mandy has been the biggest blessing to our family and loves Matt so well. It was a surprise love, so it was fitting that they had a surprise wedding. No one could have guessed it for either of them. She was in

Hollywood and he was in Dallas, but nothing gets in the way of love.

And that's what God did for you. Scripture says, before Christ, we were dead in our sins, children of wrath, slaves to sin and Satan, and enemies of God. We are not great candidates for God, who has impossibly high standards, perfect righteousness, to be in His company. Yet because of His great love and to demonstrate His love and glory, He chose the weak. He chose you.

The highest standard (God, in His moral perfection) choosing the least likely (us dead in our sin and rebellion) shows the greatest love. Highest + Least = Greatest. He loves you so much. The greatest love; that's His love for you.

This transformational truth of God choosing you in your weakness is found in 1 Corinthians 1:26–30.

> For consider your calling, brothers: not many of you were wise according to worldly standards, not many were powerful, not many were of noble birth. But God chose what is foolish in the world to shame the wise; God chose what is weak in the world to shame the strong; God chose what is low and despised in the world, even things that are not, to bring to nothing things that are, so that no human being might boast in the presence of God. And because of him you are in Christ Jesus, who became to us wisdom from God, righteousness and sanctification and redemption.

Consider who you were before God chose you. Thank Him for setting His love upon you, choosing you, and calling you His own. What a Savior.

In a position of humility, pray and ask God to keep you from your struggle for the next 24 hours.

Text or call a brother or sister in Christ to let them know if you've stayed free from your struggle for the *past* 24 hours. Tell them you're also committing, by God's strength, to staying free from your struggle/addiction for the *next* 24 hours and you'll follow up with them tomorrow to let them know if you did.

Once you have done so, initial here: _____ Date: _____

≫ **SCRIPTURE READING: Ephesians 5**

DAY 56

The Giving Tree Is Not a Living Tree

Where there is fear of God to keep the house, the enemy can find no way to enter.

St. Francis of Assisi

THERE'S A POPULAR CHILDREN'S BOOK titled *The Giving Tree* by Shel Silverstein. In it, a boy and a tree love each other. The boy comes around to see the tree, and the tree is happy. The boy swings from its branches and makes a crown

173

of leaves. The tree is happy because the boy is happy. But as time progresses, the boy comes around less. Then the boy returns and is sad. The boy wants money. The tree has no money but offers its apples to sell for money. The boy leaves with the apples, and the tree is happy because the boy is happy. Years later, the boy wants a house. The tree offers its limbs. The boy cuts the tree apart and leaves to build a house. The trunk of the tree is happy because the boy is happy. Still years later, the boy wants to sail far, far away. The tree doesn't have a boat but offers its trunk. The boy (now much older) cuts it down and sails away. The tree is happy because the boy is happy. Then finally, a decrepit older man returns, and the tree is ecstatic. But it has nothing left to offer, as it is just a stump. The old man in turn sits his wrinkly rear end on the stump of the tree. And, you guessed it, the tree is happy.

You know what I think? I think this book should be called either *How to Raise a Taker* or *A Tree's Training on Codependency*. Why? The boy was a taker. He only wanted what the tree could offer. He was in the relationship only to take for his own pleasure. The tree was horribly codependent and was happy only when the other person in the relationship was happy, even at the sake of its own livelihood.

We do this too, don't we? People ask things of us that we know aren't good ideas. They don't align with God's will, let alone our wishes. But we let them. We let them ask things of us because they force the issue or argue or escalate or are passive-aggressive. We stay in relationships longer than we should, we remain silent when we should speak, we do what we shouldn't even when the conviction of the Spirit is telling us otherwise. And we find ourselves giving ourselves away in ways we never wanted only because someone else wanted it. God doesn't want this for us. He wants us free and unhindered—from sin and from others who don't have our best in mind. It may be your boyfriend, your mom, your boss, your coworker, your roommate, your best friend, or the socialite bully. It doesn't matter. You do what God wants and live free.

God's antidote to harmful relationships is to fear God alone and no one else. This transformational truth where you are free to love and follow God without fear is found in Galatians 1:10.

> For am I now seeking the approval of man, or of God? Or am I trying to please man? If I were still trying to please man, I would not be a servant of Christ.

Consider a relationship in which you are enabling an unhealthy person to impact you in an unhealthy way, and write a prayer below asking God to give you the strength to follow Him and not that person's unhealthy demands.

_____

_____

_____

_____

_____

In a position of humility, pray and ask God to keep you from your struggle for the next 24 hours.

Text or call a brother or sister in Christ to let them know if you've stayed free from your struggle for the *past* 24 hours. Tell them you're also committing, by God's strength, to staying free from your struggle/addiction for the *next* 24 hours and you'll follow up with them tomorrow to let them know if you did.

Once you have done so, initial here: ____ Date: _____

≫ SCRIPTURE READING: Ephesians 3

DAY 57

A Friendly Foe

A Christian must never stop repenting, for I fear he never stops sinning.

Charles Spurgeon

A RANDOM ALLEY CAT lives in our neighborhood. It comes over our fence, and the kids love it. It stalks squirrels, which cracks the kids up. It'll rub up against the kids and flop on its back for them to pet its belly. It seems harmless enough and they like it, so one cold winter day, when it was catting around, we decided we'd feed it. We put out some sandwich meat and a little bowl of water.

Hill put down his hand to pet the cat, and that stinking cat bit him and wouldn't let go. It clenched on to my son's hand long enough for me to run over and shoo it away. Hill was bleeding from the two incisors that went deep between his thumb and forefinger. He was wailing, and we talked about how that cat is a bad cat and we shouldn't feed or pet it.

Well, that was two years ago, and Hill has long forgotten about the bite. And once again, my kids love the alley cat. They follow it, pet it, feed it. They think maybe this will be the time they can pet it without getting bitten or clawed. Then the cat will roll onto its back so they can pet its tummy and suddenly grip all four clawed paws into our children's arms. I hate the cat. Hate. The. Cat. I don't trust it. I've told my kids again and again not to go near it. That cat wants only what it wants and doesn't care about people.

There is a cat in your life. Scripture says Satan prowls around like a roaring lion seeking someone to devour. Any sane human being, with a warning like that, wouldn't have anything to do with Satan, but we do. We want the warmth, the feels, the attention, the companionship, the rush, the thrill, the forbidden thing, but we forget that Satan's offerings of sin are a ploy for him to pounce. We've been bitten by sin and Satan; we know the pain. But like my kids, we forget and think it won't happen like it did the last time, that maybe this time will be pleasure without pain.

Satan purrs with temptation to draw you in, then after a moment of sin's pleasure, he clenches down and cuts deep into your soul. He'll give you what you want because it's you that he wants. So the Bible says regarding this evil being: resist him. When you're suffering, lonely, bored, angry, or tired in life and just want a moment of sinful relief, resist his temptations, resist his lies, resist his offerings for rotting relief and poisonous peace. He only offers them to you because he knows your thrill means his next kill.

This transformational truth to resist Satan when he comes around to offer you the desires of the flesh is found in 1 Peter 5:8–9.

> Be sober-minded; be watchful. Your adversary the devil prowls around like a roaring lion, seeking someone to devour. Resist him, firm in your faith, knowing that the same kinds of suffering are being experienced by your brotherhood throughout the world.

Think about where you have been tempted to sin lately in your longing, suffering, and waiting, and ask God to give you the strength to resist the devil today.

In a position of humility, pray and ask God to keep you from your struggle for the next 24 hours.

Text or call a brother or sister in Christ to let them know if you've stayed free from your struggle for the *past* 24 hours. Tell them you're also committing, by God's strength, to staying free from your struggle/addiction for the *next* 24 hours and you'll follow up with them tomorrow to let them know if you did.

Once you have done so, initial here:___ Date:_____

>> **SCRIPTURE READING: 1 Peter 5**

DAY 58

My Machete

Make me what Thou wouldst have me. I bargain for nothing. I make no terms. I seek for no previous information whither Thou art taking me. I will be what Thou wilt make me, and all that Thou wilt make me. I say not, I will follow Thee whithersoever Thou goest, for I am weak, but I give myself to Thee, to lead me anywhither.

Cardinal John Henry Newman

WHEN I FIRST GOT TO HAITI in the summer of 2008, there was something culturally distinct from the US that I wasn't used to. It rattled me as I walked past people or tried talking to them in my broken Kreyòl, the Haitian language. Haiti is largely agricultural, so many people labor for their living, carrying machetes all day, every day. It was mildly sobering to stand with someone, not quite sure what they were saying, as they gestured with a two-foot sword. The orphanage I lived at backed up to a mountain, which was full of farmers and thus machetes. So a month into my stay, it was as though they might as well have been holding a garden rake, and I barely noticed the machetes anymore.

One Saturday, I took a handful of Kreyòl gospel tracts up into the mountain with a boy from the school to help with translating. We stopped along the way and handed out little Bibles to people and told them of the love of Christ. As we rounded one hill, the student stopped dead in his tracks. There were men up ahead shouting to us, and I was headed to share the gospel with them.

"Stop! We have to go back," he pleaded.

"Why? Let's take them Bibles."

"No, we have to go back right now." He was already walking backward.

"Why? Let's go see them."

He said, "The men are saying that if you come one step closer, they'll chop you up."

"Oh. Say, uh, we should probably go." I might have run.

Why the story about machetes? Machetes aren't bad; they are amoral, neither good nor bad. They're inanimate objects. What matters is the heart of the person holding the machete.

Haitians are incredible people. They are resilient, loving, passionate, resourceful, hardworking, and full of love. The same thing could happen to me in Dallas, but with guns instead of machetes. The point isn't that Haitians have machetes. The point is, how are you using your "machete"—meaning the tool God gave you, which is your body? Are you using it for good, for productivity, for life, for help? Or are you using it to hurt, to threaten, to take from others?

God instructs us that our bodies used to be tools for unrighteousness. Our hearts were sinful, so we used our bodies in harmful ways against ourselves and others. But now, yielded and yoked to Christ, our bodies are instruments of righteousness, meant to bring about a harvest—a harvest of souls for God's unending kingdom.

How will you use your machete today? Will you put bad things in your body? Will you use your body for sexual sin? Lies and deceit? Pride and arrogance? Will you spend money, starve your body, and concern yourself with outward beauty? Or will you use your body, your speech, your time, your money, your mind, your very soul for righteousness? It's a daily decision. Decide now. Be a tool in His hands for the harvest.

This transformational truth is found in Romans 6:13.

> Do not present your members to sin as instruments for unrighteousness, but present yourselves to God as those who have been brought from death to life, and your members to God as instruments for righteousness.

Write a prayer below presenting your body to God today as an instrument of righteousness. Make no threats, and do not use it for harm.

In a position of humility, pray and ask God to keep you from your struggle for the next 24 hours.

Text or call a brother or sister in Christ to let them know if you've stayed free from your struggle for the *past* 24 hours. Tell them you're also committing, by God's strength, to staying free from your struggle/addiction for the *next* 24 hours and you'll follow up with them tomorrow to let them know if you did.

Once you have done so, initial here: ____ Date: _____

>> **SCRIPTURE READING: 1 Peter 4**

DAY 59

Through, Not Around

The Lord gets his best soldiers out of the highlands of affliction.

Charles Spurgeon

BEFORE I GOT TO SUDAN in the summer of 2009, we had a multiday layover in northern Uganda, so we decided to float the Nile at Jinja. Now, as with all of life, expectations are everything. And every Bible movie I've ever seen depicts a slow-moving, peaceful, reed-lined Nile.

We arrived at the launch camp, purchased our day passes, got fitted for life vests and helmets, and were placed with a group of strangers. Then Sally, our guide, gave us the basics, shared what to do when we fall out (I noted she didn't say "if"), and told us that our lives would depend on following her instructions (I sheepishly looked around to make sure everyone caught that last bit of info). Before boarding, I asked, "Are there Nile crocodiles in this stretch?" She off-handedly replied, "We don't see them." Right, not exactly reassuring.

We carried the rubber raft to the Nile and, sure enough, calm as could be. But less than an hour in, things changed. The calm became rapids, and calm Sally was now yelling, "Left! Paddle right! Paddle hard, straight!"

But it was Sally's strategy that surprised me the most. She didn't go around the rapids. In fact, she purposely took us straight into them. She would shout, "Paddle for the V!" where the rapids seemed to converge and were the absolute worst. During a smooth stretch, I asked her, "What's the reason for going through the roughest patch? More adventure?" She replied with confusing-to-me certainty, "So we don't flip." She continued, "The other parts look calmer, but that's where the rocks are. If we try to go around them, we'll get stuck on the rocks, the river will overwhelm us, and we'll capsize. You can't go around them; you have to go through them."

When we approached the Class IV and V rapids (very high, not amateur gradings), I wasn't surprised that our captain took us weak and unexperienced rafters straight toward and through them. We grew stronger, braver, more secure in our captain, and tighter as a team. And I no longer feared the rapids; instead, I respected and trusted our captain.

God does just this. When the suffering, affliction, trials, testing, and persecution of life come, He doesn't usually take us around them. He confidently takes us through them,

182

with a somewhat inexperienced crew around us. And as He does, we, too, grow stronger, more courageous, more like Christ, more certain that He is a captain worth trusting. The pain is never in vain. When the trials come, trust Christ. He's going to take you through them, and afterward you will fear and revere Him alone instead of the passing river of testing.

This powerful promise that God is at work in your suffering and trials to produce something far greater in you is found in James 1:2–4.

> Count it all joy, my brothers, when you meet trials of various kinds, for you know that the testing of your faith produces steadfastness. And let steadfastness have its full effect, that you may be perfect and complete, lacking in nothing.

Consider a time of testing you have been through or are in. Thank God that He is taking you through it and not around it, and praise Him that regardless of the class of the rapids, He is a captain worth your trust and is at work producing powerful things in you. .

In a position of humility, pray and ask God to keep you from your struggle for the next 24 hours.

Text or call a brother or sister in Christ to let them know if you've stayed free from your struggle for the *past* 24 hours.

Tell them you're also committing, by God's strength, to staying free from your struggle/addiction for the *next* 24 hours and you'll follow up with them tomorrow to let them know if you did.

Once you have done so, initial here: ___ Date: _____

>> **SCRIPTURE READING: 1 Peter 1**

DAY 60

Band-Aid, Not Band Shame

Anybody who lives beneath the Cross and who has discerned in the Cross of Jesus the utter wickedness of all men and of his own heart will find there is no sin that can ever be alien to him. Anybody who has once been horrified by the dreadfulness of his own sin that nailed Jesus to the Cross will no longer be horrified by even the rankest sins of a brother.

Dietrich Bonhoeffer

WITH OUR YOUNG KIDS, cuts and scrapes are part of daily life, so we have a steady stock of Band-Aids in the house (only exacerbated by Penny, who wears them as fashion accessories). Our kids will be out riding bikes or climbing the tree fort, only to come running into the house crying because of some cut. They see blood, and it demands a Band-Aid. I think these Band-Aids have a psychological and emotional effect, because as soon as that covering goes on, the tears turn off. If only life as an adult were so simple.

You know what I don't say when my kids come running with a cut? "You know better!" I don't shame them for being hurt. Instead, I clean their cut and give them a Band-Aid. They didn't mean to get hurt. And even if they were doing something they shouldn't have been when they got hurt, the time to talk or discipline is later. A cut is a time for covering. After all, they're called Band-Aids, not Band-Shames.

But somewhere along the way as we age, we get embarrassed by our accidents, our sin. We hide them, and they get infected. One reason why we do this is because when we've gone to others to tell them about our accident or pain, we've gotten shamed instead of aided. We've gotten lectured instead of loved.

God didn't design us to live like that. The body of Christ is to give Band-Aids, to be a place of healing, and to carry one another's burdens (meaning everyone has them, and if you aren't going to others, it is not because you aren't accident-prone or given to sin but rather because you're proud or wounded).

I used to use alcohol as my Band-Aid. Now, I use Christ and the community of believers He's given me—Laura, Mike, Shane, JP, Marshall. They give me aid and remind me of the covering of Jesus's grace, not shame.

This transformational truth to care for one another and run to the body of Christ when afflicted is found in Galatians 6:1–2.

> Brothers, if anyone is caught in any transgression, you who are spiritual should restore him in a spirit of gentleness. Keep watch on yourself, lest you too be tempted. Bear one another's burdens, and so fulfill the law of Christ.

What is a pain in your life that you haven't taken to another believer so they can cover you, albeit imperfectly, with

185

the love of God and lighten your burden? Write it down and take it to God. Ask Him for someone to confess your sin to.

_____

_____

_____

_____

_____

In a position of humility, pray and ask God to keep you from your struggle for the next 24 hours.

Text or call a brother or sister in Christ to let them know if you've stayed free from your struggle for the *past* 24 hours. Tell them you're also committing, by God's strength, to staying free from your struggle/addiction for the *next* 24 hours and you'll follow up with them tomorrow to let them know if you did.

Once you have done so, initial here: _____ Date: _____

⟫ SCRIPTURE READING: 1 Peter 2

PRAISE GOD! You are now sixty days into your new habit of daily deciding to war against sin by the power of the Spirit and by trusting the Word of God in fellowship with His people. This path to freedom is yielding much fruit in your life. Just look at the freedom that has come during the last two months! God is on the move. Remain steadfast; He is doing a great work in you.

DAY 61

Laura's Cavities

Pardon comes not to the soul alone, or rather, Christ comes not to the soul with pardon only; it is that which He opens the door and enters by, but He comes with a Spirit of life and power.

John Owen

LAURA BRUSHES HER TEETH multiple times a day, flosses, has a little dental pick thing, and uses mouthwash. If it's good dental hygiene, she's doing it. And this is benefited by the fact that she's more of a salty snack person and would take buffalo wings over ice cream any day of the week. So it was surprising when the other day she went to the dentist and had three cavities. You read that right—three.

Three cavities is what you get in the third grade when you don't brush your teeth for a month and live off sour gummies, chocolate, and donuts. But yet here she is a grown adult, with excellent hygiene, whose teeth are in bad shape. Want to know the culprit? Hippy toothpaste. She was using that nothing-bad-for-you toothpaste; well, the inverse is true too—there's nothing good in it for you either. She might as well have been rubbing peanut butter on her teeth each night. It offered her zero protection. While she was doing all the right things and had all the right habits, without the power of fluoride, she was riddled with decay.

And likewise, we, too, are subject to spiritual decay. We are religious creatures by nature. We think in our brokenness we can work our way to God or earn his favor by doing the right things. We try to brush the sin off by doing all the right things and having all the right habits. We weren't saved by works, and we will not be sanctified by works. We have to have the power of the Holy Spirit at work in us to keep us from spiritual decay. He, not the right religious habits, is the protection against decay. The Pharisees were great at cultivating the right habits, but they didn't have any power against sin, because they didn't have a relationship with God.

So don't just go through the motions of Bible study, prayer, Scripture memory, or even this book, apart from a total dependence on and relationship with the one true God. His Spirit will keep you from moral and spiritual decay.

This powerful promise that God's Spirit saved you and will continue sanctifying you is found in Galatians 3:2–3.

> Let me ask you only this: Did you receive the Spirit by works of the law or by hearing with faith? Are you so foolish? Having begun by the Spirit, are you now being perfected by the flesh?

Think about all your faith-based activities. Then decide today that you will not engage in any of them out of religious routine. Ask God to be at work through each of the things you do, whether Bible reading, prayer, worship, serving, et al.

_____

_____

_____

_____

_____

In a position of humility, pray and ask God to keep you from your struggle for the next 24 hours.

Text or call a brother or sister in Christ to let them know if you've stayed free from your struggle for the *past* 24 hours. Tell them you're also committing, by God's strength, to staying free from your struggle/addiction for the *next* 24 hours and you'll follow up with them tomorrow to let them know if you did.

Once you have done so, initial here: ____ Date: _____

>> **SCRIPTURE READING: Psalm 51**

DAY 62

God's Not Fair

Sanctified afflictions are spiritual promotions.
John Dod

I LIVE WITH A LAWYER, and thus I have a lot of arguments and lose many of them. His name is Hill, and he's seven years old. He has a photographic memory and incredible logic. He truly lawyers me about treats, screen time, you name it, and standing on his strong sense of right and wrong, he demands, "That isn't fair." When he says this, I respond, "You're right; it's not fair. And trust me, you don't want me to make things fair." Then we have a conversation about grace (getting what you don't deserve) and mercy (not getting what you do deserve).

And I've come to realize and be really grateful that God actually isn't fair. It seems crazy to say that a perfectly righteous

189

and holy God isn't fair. Kinda sounds blasphemous. Unless you understand this: if He were "fair," we would be eternally separated from Him due to our sin. Fair would mean giving me what I deserve: judgment and hell. Unlike my son and me, on most days, fair is not what we want from God. And thankfully, He's not fair. Make no mistake; He is just and disciplines His children, but He is also full of grace, mercy, love, and gentleness.

Some of us (I know from experience) think that because of our past, God is not able to or will not bless our present or future. There will be no kids because of my past abortion. No more love in my future because of my divorce. No guy will love me because of my sexual past. No woman will love me because I struggle with same-sex attraction. No one will hire me because of my record. No one will ever trust me because of my past addiction. And while He likely won't give you every single thing you want, He'll give you so much more than you deserve and exactly what you need for life and godliness. Thank God that he literally is not fair.

This powerful promise that God doesn't treat us fairly is in Psalm 103:10.

> He does not deal with us according to our sins, nor repay us according to our iniquities. (The NIV says, "He does not treat us as our sins deserve.")

Thank God right now that He doesn't treat you as you deserve for certain sins you've committed. Cry out with gratitude that instead of wrath, because of Jesus, you got love, mercy, blessing, and hope.

In a position of humility, pray and ask God to keep you from your struggle for the next 24 hours.

Text or call a brother or sister in Christ to let them know if you've stayed free from your struggle for the *past* 24 hours. Tell them you're also committing, by God's strength, to staying free from your struggle/addiction for the *next* 24 hours and you'll follow up with them tomorrow to let them know if you did.

Once you have done so, initial here: ____ Date: _____

>> **SCRIPTURE READING: Psalm 103**

DAY 63

Dad in the Darkness

If God is present at every point in space, if we cannot go where He is not, cannot even conceive of a place where He is not, why then has not that Presence become the one universally celebrated fact of the world? . . . Men do not know that God is here. What a difference it would make if they knew.

A. W. Tozer

I REMEMBER IN LATE DECEMBER 2005, after my family had an intervention for me, we were all staying at my brother

191

and sister-in-law's house in Dallas. It was three stories, and I was staying in the office on the first floor. I was painfully and miserably sober against my will, and I'm sure very unpleasant to be around. I couldn't sleep, and when I did, I had horrific nightmares. I was a flight risk, and my family was keeping very close tabs on me.

I'll never forget one night I was lying there miserable, lonely, depressed, and haunted by what I had done to my own life when the door to my room opened. It startled me, and I just waited. Then slowly a person lay down beside me on the floor. It was my dad. He had come from his warm, comfortable bedroom to sleep on the blow-up mattress beside me. Later he told me he was afraid I was going to leave and go out drinking, so he came to stay beside me. I'll always remember that night my dad stood guard over me and over the evil that was fighting for my soul and my life.

And God does the same for you.

In one of my favorite passages of Scripture, Psalm 34, there is an incredible verse that says Jesus, named here as *the* angel of the Lord, encamps around God's people. Like my dad did for me, God does for you. He loves you. He stands guard over you. You are His, and He fights on your behalf. So, rest well tonight—the angel of the Lord is encamped around you.

This powerful promise that Jesus encamps around those who fear Him is found in Psalm 34:7.

The angel of the LORD encamps around those who fear Him.

Close your eyes and picture this reality. Now, thank God for the fact that He watches and stands guard over you.

In a position of humility, pray and ask God to keep you from your struggle for the next 24 hours.

Text or call a brother or sister in Christ to let them know if you've stayed free from your struggle for the *past* 24 hours. Tell them you're also committing, by God's strength, to staying free from your struggle/addiction for the *next* 24 hours and you'll follow up with them tomorrow to let them know if you did.

Once you have done so, initial here: _____ Date: _____

>> **SCRIPTURE READING: Psalm 73**

DAY 64

The Secret Killer

In the presence of a Christian brother, I can dare to be a sinner.
Dietrich Bonhoeffer

EVERYONE HAS SECRETS. Secrets they are deathly ashamed of. And in our shame of what we've done or what was done to us, we think, *I'm going to take this secret to the grave.* We think that if we just hide it until we die, we can keep it from hurting us or others or having any consequences as a result. But the problem with these secrets we want to take to the grave is that they, in fact, are the ones taking *you* to the grave.

The abuse you suffered, the person you abused, the addiction you hide, the abortion from your college days, the infidelity from that one trip, the prostitute, the theft, the videos and photos you still have of your ex that they don't even know about, the money they forgot that you owe, the thing you did while they were passed out, the secret hatred you have for that person, the same-sex lust you have for another man while married with kids, that friend at work who is becoming more than a friend, the porn and masturbation struggle you've never told a soul about, the pills you take, the app you download then delete, the browser history you clear, the self-starving—you know your secret. And so does Satan. And truth be told, your secret sin is killing you. Numbers 32:23 says that "your sin will find you out." Satan will use these secrets to condemn you, shame you, drive you to hide from God, and make you hate yourself. And like Judas, you will not take your secret to the grave; it will take you there.

But there is another who is a secret killer. Jesus. Because with Jesus, there is forgiveness, cleansing, a new identity, righteousness, light. So, be humble and thus be free. Confess your secret to Jesus and a fellow believer in Jesus. He will kill your secret and destroy its power over you as you bring it into the light. Do it today and be free.

> Blessed is the man against whom the LORD counts no
> iniquity,
> and in whose spirit there is no deceit.
>
> For when I kept silent, my bones wasted away
> through my groaning all day long.

For day and night your hand was heavy upon me;
　　my strength was dried up as by the heat of
　　　summer.

I acknowledged my sin to you,
　　and I did not cover my iniquity;
I said, "I will confess my transgressions to the LORD,"
　　and you forgave the iniquity of my sin. (Ps. 32:2–5)

Did the Lord bring a secret to your mind as you read? Write your prayer of confession to Him and call your daily accountability partner to confess it to them. Thank God for the freedom of walking in the light.

_____

_____

_____

_____

_____

In a position of humility, pray and ask God to keep you from your struggle for the next 24 hours.

Text or call a brother or sister in Christ to let them know if you've stayed free from your struggle for the *past* 24 hours. Tell them you're also committing, by God's strength, to staying free from your struggle/addiction for the *next* 24 hours and you'll follow up with them tomorrow to let them know if you did.

Once you have done so, initial here: ____ Date: _____

≫ SCRIPTURE READING: Psalm 32

DAY 65

Poor Dressing or a Rich Blessing

The Bible has told me a great many of my faults; it would tell you yours if you would let it.

Charles Spurgeon

I WANT TO TELL YOU ABOUT my pajamas. Don't envision some nice button-down designer pajamas. Picture a ten-year-old black Fruit of the Loom hoodie and some old scrubs I got from Walmart. We're talking baby spit-up, diaper-cream-streaked, kids'-snot-they-wipe-on-me pajamas. And sidenote—I'm also the kind of guy whose day doesn't start until I shower.

But one particular day, I didn't shower. I stayed in my pajamas, looked at my bed hair in the mirror, and headed to church. I got mic'ed up to teach, and as soon as the worship music ended, I walked up onstage in my nasty pajamas, bed hair, and ratty loafers.

People looked at me like I had lost my mind. One guy to this day still says he can't get the image out of his head; he truly thought I was in bad shape and sleep-deprived with babies in the house. But it was all intentional. I purposely looked in the mirror at what was left of my disheveled hair, didn't brush my teeth, stayed in my pajamas, and left home to preach through James. I didn't do this because I was running late or had been up all night caring for baby Penny; I did it because that's exactly how we often live our lives.

We look into the mirror of God's Word; it shows us what is out of place, unkempt, and off. Yet if we see the wrongs and do not yield ourselves to the Spirit for Him to cleanse and correct them, we are posers in pajamas. Conversely, James says, when you look into the perfect Word and yield your life to it, you will be a blessing. Because God's ways lead to life and peace (Rom. 8:6)—not just in your life but even more so in the lives of others. That was entirely on purpose.

This powerful promise that you, as you conform to the Word of God, will be a blessing is found in James 1:23–25.

> For if anyone is a hearer of the word and not a doer, he is like a man who looks intently at his natural face in a mirror. For he looks at himself and goes away and at once forgets what he was like. But the one who looks into the perfect law, the law of liberty, and perseveres, being no hearer who forgets but a doer who acts, he will be blessed in his doing.

Consider one way your life does not reflect the mirror of God's Word, and instead of seeing it and doing nothing to change it, ask the Spirit of God to change, cleanse, and correct it in you today. He lives to do so.

In a position of humility, pray and ask God to keep you from your struggle for the next 24 hours.

Text or call a brother or sister in Christ to let them know if you've stayed free from your struggle for the *past* 24 hours. Tell them you're also committing, by God's strength, to staying free from your struggle/addiction for the *next* 24 hours and you'll follow up with them tomorrow to let them know if you did.

Once you have done so, initial here: _____ Date: _____

>> **SCRIPTURE READING: Psalm 1**

DAY 66

Church Every Day

There are many persons who think Sunday is a sponge with which to wipe out the sins of the week.

Henry Ward Beecher

GRADUATING FROM COLLEGE as a functional alcoholic, I clearly wasn't much for studying. School got in the way of my drinking. So when it came time for finals, it was all-night cramming. I remember staying up for three nights in a row my junior year, committing information to short-term memory, taking a test, and repeating the cycle. I got the grades, then lost the information, but I'll never forget hallucinating the third night from sleep deprivation. My mind was confused and telling me things were there when they weren't. It was a state of confusion and deception.

Certain daily necessities are required for a healthy existence. Sleep, water, and food are needed daily for our bodies to operate well and not shut down. We can possibly go a day or so without these, but try to do more than that and things start to get bad pretty quickly.

Most people sleep seven nights a week, yet most of us go to church once a week and live in a state of confusion and deception the other six days. "Wait," you say. "Are you telling me I have to be *in* church seven days a week?" No. I'm telling you that you have to be *with* church seven days a week. Actually, I'm not; God is.

God warns us that if we are not encouraged by the people of God every single day, we will be hardened by the deceitfulness of sin. Just like you require sleep every single day or you'll be confused and deceived, even seeing things that do not exist, we are to be encouraged by one another daily. Otherwise, our hearts (meaning our spirits) will be hardened by the lies of sin.

I text with members of my community group (men and women I walk through life with) daily. When I'm tempted by alcohol, the lies usually sound like this: *You were more fun when you drank* or *You're so serious now, and nobody wants to hang out with the serious, somber guy* or *Stress wasn't so heavy when you drank. You could have one drink and it wouldn't be a problem.*

Knowing that I can daily be deceived by sin, I confess even my temptations. One friend, JP, is always quick to say, "That stuff is death." And Laura says, "John, if you drink, it will kill you. Those are lies. It never made your life better."

The lies continue: *But some people drink and they're fine. The Bible doesn't say not to drink; it just says don't be drunk.* But Laura's and JP's counsel isn't for everyone who can drink without getting drunk; it's for me. And for me, every time I drank, I got drunk. For me, it is nothing but death and loss. And in that moment, I need someone clear-minded to remind me of the truth in the fog of sin's lies. Because sin's full-time job is to deceive us, harden our hearts, lure us in—and its aim is death. God's antidote to the daily lies of sin is the daily encouragement from God's people.

Church on Sunday is good; it just isn't sufficient. Don't take my word for it, take God at His Word.

This powerful promise that other believers' daily encouragement will keep you from sin's lies is found in Hebrews 3:13.

> But exhort one another every day, as long as it is called "today," that none of you may be hardened by the deceitfulness of sin.

Pray and ask God which other believers you should start a daily "truths of God" text thread with. Confess your temptations to one another and dispel the lies with God's truth. Thank God for this provision.

_____

_____

_____

_____

_____

In a position of humility, pray and ask God to keep you from your struggle for the next 24 hours.

Text or call a brother or sister in Christ to let them know if you've stayed free from your struggle for the *past* 24 hours. Tell them you're also committing, by God's strength, to staying free from your struggle/addiction for the *next* 24 hours and you'll follow up with them tomorrow to let them know if you did.

Once you have done so, initial here: ____ Date: _____

» SCRIPTURE READING: Hebrews 3

DAY 67

Asleep at the Keel

The Spirit's message to us is never, "Look at me; listen to me; come to me; get to know me," but always, "Look at *him*, and see *his* glory; listen to *him* and hear his word; go to *him*, and have life; get to know *him*, and taste his gift of joy and peace." The Spirit, we might say, is the matchmaker, the celestial marriage broker, whose role it is to bring us and Christ together and ensure that we stay together.

J. I. Packer

THREE MONTHS AFTER everything fell apart, and two months after surrendering my life to Jesus, I was invited to go to Europe by Jeff, one of my clients and good friends. His wife couldn't go, so he gave me her ticket. It was hilarious to be with people from his company and all their spouses, and me as his plus-one. We shared rooms in every town with two beds side by side. At this time in my life, I had lost everything, but I had Jesus.

He would laugh and tell everyone how I slept throughout the trip. When it was time for bed, I would lie down on my back, hands across my chest, and in his words, "Sleep like a baby." It baffled him, given the state of my life, but it didn't baffle me; I had all the peace in the world. Anxiety, pressure, stress, and confusion should have weighed me down, but I had Jesus and slept in peace every night. But with my life falling apart, it appeared I was asleep at the wheel.

Jesus slept in a storm of life too. One night with His disciples, He was crossing the Sea of Galilee when a massive storm came upon them. These trained fishermen were certain they were going to die. They rushed to the back of the boat to find

Jesus asleep on a pillow in the middle of this torrent (Mark 4:35–41). How could He sleep at such a perilous, chaotic, life-threatening time? How could He be asleep at the keel?

Because He knew God's Word, the prophecies about Him, and how He would die. And He knew He wouldn't go down in the sea; He was going up on a cross. This wasn't His time and wouldn't be the disciples' either. And in that, there is peace.

God has ordained every single day of your life. Truth be told, there is no such thing as an accidental death. You have been given a life with a fixed number of days, fixed by God. And in that, there is a supernatural peace. A peace that surpasses human understanding. Don't fear. Jesus is with you. Your days are numbered and will not be shortened. God is your Provider, your Healer, your Shepherd, your Strength, and your Peace. If He slept in the storm, so can you. Be faithful during the day and sleep well at night. Storms are certain, but no storm lasts forever. God does. And He is the Keeper of your soul.

This powerful promise and truth that God has ordained the number of your days as your Creator and Sustainer is found in Psalm 139:16.

> Your eyes saw my unformed substance;
> in your book were written, every one of them,
>   the days that were formed for me,
>   when as yet there was none of them.

Consider what storm you are in. Pray and ask God to give you peace that your life is in His hands and not at the mercy of the waves or the downpours of life's storms.

_____

_____

_____

In a position of humility, pray and ask God to keep you from your struggle for the next 24 hours.

Text or call a brother or sister in Christ to let them know if you've stayed free from your struggle for the *past* 24 hours. Tell them you're also committing, by God's strength, to staying free from your struggle/addiction for the *next* 24 hours and you'll follow up with them tomorrow to let them know if you did.

Once you have done so, initial here: ____ Date: _____

>> **SCRIPTURE READING: Psalm 139**

DAY 68

How to Win Every Argument

Be not angry that you cannot make others as you wish them to be since you cannot make yourself as you wish to be.

Thomas à Kempis

I'M MARRIED, AND THUS I ARGUE. It's such an odd thing. The person I love the most is the person I argue with the most. Or at least I used to. I don't anymore. Because I have learned the secret of how to win every single argument.

Think about a tug-of-war. I'm on one end and Laura's on the other. When she tugs on the rope, I can drag her harder and faster over to my side by arguing points and undoing the strength in her logic. But the problem with this is that when I "win an argument" with Laura, I don't win. She's hurt, and I'm a prideful jerk. Pulling someone over to your side isn't winning; it's bullying. And you might "win" the argument, but you'll lose the relationship.

The way to win an argument is to drop the rope.

I didn't make this up; God did. I read it in His Word one day, and it has transformed my marriage. At one point in time, we had three kids, three and under. The stress, pressure, and demands were unrelenting, and we quarreled a ton. It was exhausting, and no matter how many arguments I won, the quality of our relationship was being lost. So I decided, *Well, God delivered me from alcoholism; He can probably deliver me from arguing with my wife.* And He has.

Now, every time (okay, most times—I'm still very much in progress too) I feel the tug on the relational rope, rather than pulling harder to get her to my way of thinking, I drop the rope of the argument and instead move toward her, emotionally and physically. In arguments, I stop my proud logic and move to embrace her. It's changed our whole marriage. My next challenge will be to do this with my kids. Pray for me in that.

This transformational truth that we can drop the tug-of-war rope in relationships and the quarreling will cease is found in Proverbs 17:14.

> The beginning of strife is like letting out water,
> so quit before the quarrel breaks out.

Who is the person you argue with the most? Your room-mate, boss, parent, spouse, child? Write a prayer below asking God to help you drop the rope when you feel the tug and give you the strength, love, and humility to instead move toward the person.

_____

_____

_____

_____

_____

In a position of humility, pray and ask God to keep you from your struggle for the next 24 hours.

Text or call a brother or sister in Christ to let them know if you've stayed free from your struggle for the *past* 24 hours. Tell them you're also committing, by God's strength, to staying free from your struggle/addiction for the *next* 24 hours and you'll follow up with them tomorrow to let them know if you did.

Once you have done so, initial here: _____ Date: _____

>> **SCRIPTURE READING: Proverbs 17**

DAY 69

Enlist the Arborist

The tragedy of life and of the world is not that men do not know God; the tragedy is that, knowing Him, they still insist on going their own way.

William Barclay

WE HAVE A HUGE TEXAS LIVE OAK in our backyard. It's an amazing gift to our children and shades them from the summer sun and heat. The problem is, it extends over our house and has massive limbs that could crush bedrooms if they fell in a storm. So I had an arborist out one day. I asked him to give me a quote to trim back the tree. It was way more than I could pay just for that one tree (so I later got a polesaw for one-fourth of the price and took care of it myself), but before he left, he said, "Well, let's check the front yard and see what needs to be done there." I agreed, even though I knew I couldn't afford it.

As we walked to the front, he stopped, pointed to a bush on the side of our house, and said, "Whoa! What are you going to do about THAT?!" I sarcastically shot back, "Um, water it?" Without missing a beat, he replied, "Don't water that. It'll destroy your house. Soon your drywall will start cracking, your doors won't shut right, and the foundation will shift." Well, he got my attention with that. Having never set foot in our house, he had just described our ceiling, garage door, and kitchen. He proceeded to tell me the bush was actually an oak tree, probably grown from an acorn that a squirrel (a rat with a fluffy tail) buried and forgot to collect. He was right. That bush I had been watering was in fact a tree that was destroying my house.

Sin in our lives is like that. It's something seemingly harmless, so we water and cultivate it, but don't correlate the fact that it is indeed the thing that is destroying our house, our soul, our relationships, our foundation in Christ.

I have chainsawed that tree down two times. And yet it keeps sprouting back up. The only way to truly get rid of it is to uproot it, but the problem is, I'm not strong enough and thus haven't. Same with your sin. Establishing some boundaries, rules, or ways to cut it back won't prevail. God must uproot the idol buried within your heart. And the Spirit alone can do the uprooting; you're not strong enough. Will you ask Him to?

This transformational truth that we must kill idols before they kill us is found in John 15:2.

> Every branch in me that does not bear fruit he takes away, and every branch that does bear fruit he prunes, that it may bear more fruit.

What is one of your idols (a sin you love and serve and give yourself to)? Write a prayer below forsaking it and asking God to do anything and everything necessary to uproot it from your life.

In a position of humility, pray and ask God to keep you from your struggle for the next 24 hours.

Text or call a brother or sister in Christ to let them know if you've stayed free from your struggle for the *past* 24 hours. Tell them you're also committing, by God's strength, to staying free from your struggle/addiction for the *next* 24 hours and you'll follow up with them tomorrow to let them know if you did.

Once you have done so, initial here: ____ Date: _____

>> **SCRIPTURE READING: Colossians 1**

DAY 70

Useful to the Master

No man ever became holy by chance. There must be a resolve, a desire, a panting, a pining after obedience to God, or else we shall never have it.

Charles Spurgeon

GROWING UP, my dad was always doing projects in the garage. I was fascinated by all the different tools, saws, wrenches, and drivers. He'd let me build things, take things apart, and use his equipment. Now that I'm a dad, I have tools of my own. And in particular, I have a few different socket sets. One set is pristine, each socket in its place, wrenches clean, in good condition, and ready for use. Another set is older, covered in grime, and randomly tossed into an old can. Guess which one I use most?

God says we are like that. He longs to use us for His work. I remember, after trusting in Christ, having a deep yearning to be used by God. I was newly sober, and after years of squandering my life, I was so eager and hopeful that God might use me for something or someone. So I prayed and watched for Him. I read the Bible and learned about Him. I got on my knees daily and pleaded with Him to take away my addictions and sin patterns. I changed the music I listened to and started singing worship music. I was changing because He was changing me. He was ordering my life and cleansing me from my sin.

As a worldly, materialistic, foolish drunk, I was like that random collection of old sockets—not worthless, but not super useful in my condition. The Master took me and rearranged me, cleansed me by the blood of Jesus, and restored me. He was preparing me for good works (Eph. 2:8–10).

The Bible says God is our Master and longs to use us in His miraculous plan to rescue the world from sin and death. But to be useful, we must be ready. Ask God to get you ready. Put away sin and put on godliness. Soon you'll find there is no greater adventure or life than one devoted to God's kingdom work, His glory, and to laboring by His power. Get yourself ready, because God is longing to put you to great use.

This powerful promise that as we are cleansed from sin and struggles, we become useful to the Master is found in 2 Timothy 2:20–21.

> Now in a great house there are not only vessels of gold and silver but also of wood and clay, some for honorable use, some for dishonorable. Therefore, if anyone cleanses himself from what is dishonorable, he will be a vessel for honorable use, set apart as holy, useful to the master of the house, ready for every good work.

Write a prayer below asking God to reveal to you what area of your life needs cleaning and reordering to be of greater use to Him for the kingdom.

_____

_____

_____

_____

In a position of humility, pray and ask God to keep you from your struggle for the next 24 hours.

Text or call a brother or sister in Christ to let them know if you've stayed free from your struggle for the *past* 24 hours. Tell them you're also committing, by God's strength, to staying free from your struggle/addiction for the *next* 24 hours and you'll follow up with them tomorrow to let them know if you did.

Once you have done so, initial here: _____ Date: _____

>> **SCRIPTURE READING: 1 Timothy 2**

DAY 71

Surrounding Matter Matters

Christian brotherhood is not an ideal which we must realize; it is rather a reality created by God in Christ in which we may participate. The more clearly we learn to recognize that the ground and strength and promise of all our fellowship is in Jesus Christ alone, the more serenely shall we think of our fellowship and pray and hope for it.

Dietrich Bonhoeffer

WHILE LIVING IN HAITI that one summer, I saw Pastor Henri growing mango seedlings in old coffee cans. Turns out, he had a few reasons for doing so. He could control the watering needs of the young plants. He could also ensure that the young plants would grow stronger in rich soil conditions. Some of the land close to the sea struggles to grow anything because of the high salt content in the soil. It's dry and hard, and the salinity is too high.

Surroundings matter when something is trying to grow.

You may be in this place. I know I once was there, and frankly always will be. I drank hard for twelve years, and my life revolved around alcohol. To get well, I had to change some things, including my environment and influences. And don't get me wrong, I was the worst influence on everyone. But if nothing changed, nothing was going to change. So I stopped going to bars and started going to recovery meetings and church. I stopped downing alcohol and started ingesting the Bible. I stopped some relationships—some really close ones that weren't helping me get and stay sober. And I started some relationships with people who would help and encourage me in this new growth with God. I was a young believer, and God dropped me into a coffee can with the rich soil of godly friendships, some living water from the Holy Spirit, and a church where my roots could grow deep.

If you don't have godly friendships, a daily relationship with God, and a Christ-centered church that's healthy and biblical, it's time to ask God to drop you into a coffee can and give you a season of growth. Because, as with anything that's trying to grow, surroundings matter.

This transformational truth that who you are around affects your life and health is found in 1 Corinthians 15:33–34.

Do not be deceived: "Bad company ruins good morals." Wake up from your drunken stupor, as is right, and do not go on sinning.

Write out a prayer either thanking God for the good surroundings He's given you or asking Him to give you new surroundings. If you don't have any Christian friends or a church, ask God to lead you to them, and make plans to attend church this weekend or call one today. Your growth depends on it.

_____

_____

_____

_____

_____

In a position of humility, pray and ask God to keep you from your struggle for the next 24 hours.

Text or call a brother or sister in Christ to let them know if you've stayed free from your struggle for the *past* 24 hours. Tell them you're also committing, by God's strength, to staying free from your struggle/addiction for the *next* 24 hours and you'll follow up with them tomorrow to let them know if you did.

Once you have done so, initial here: _____ Date: _____

›› SCRIPTURE READING: 1 Corinthians 15

DAY 72

Little Refinement in Confinement

The Christian knows also of a relationship far more intimate than that general relationship of man to man and it is for this more intimate relationship that he reserves the term "brother." The true brotherhood, according to Christian teaching, is the brotherhood of the redeemed.

J. Gresham Machen

TO MY SHOCK, after years of drunk driving, the only times I have ever been behind bars has been for ministry. I have shared the gospel and led Bible studies in prison. Prison life can be pretty rough. If you haven't ever been inside a prison, it's often crammed with cells of bunkbeds, zero personal space, and even totally exposed showers and toilets. Privacy is a unicorn in prison—unless you are placed in solitary confinement. Solitary confinement at first glance might sound like a great escape from being crammed together with all the other inmates. But the truth is, it's the worst place in any prison. In solitary confinement, body, soul, and mind wither away. And the reason is because human beings were made to be in the company of others. A solitary cell is a living hell.

Yet in the spiritual life, people often place themselves in spiritual solitary confinement, thinking, *It's just me and God, and all is good.* But it's not. A human alone is a human undone. God gave us the body of Christ, of which we are a part and of which Jesus is the head, for us to thrive (Eph. 1:22–23). And apart from the body of Christ, that being a local church, you are in spiritual solitary confinement. And in spiritual solitary confinement, there is no refinement (Prov. 27:17). No sanctification. No growing to be more like Christ. No fanning into flame your gifts. No encouragement from and to the saints. Living separate and not being a part of a local church is to wither in body, soul, and mind. If you don't have any Christian friends or a church, ask God to lead you to them and make plans to attend a church this weekend or call one today; your life depends on it.

This transformational truth that we are part of the body of Christ and must remain so is found in 1 Corinthians 12:19–21.

> If all were a single member, where would the body be? As it is, there are many parts, yet one body. The eye cannot say to the hand, "I have no need of you," nor again the head to the feet, "I have no need of you."

Confess to God in prayer the areas of life where you feel you are isolated. Ask Him to show you if this has been self-imposed and what one next step could be.

In a position of humility, pray and ask God to keep you from your struggle for the next 24 hours.

Text or call a brother or sister in Christ to let them know if you've stayed free from your struggle for the *past* 24 hours. Tell them you're also committing, by God's strength, to staying free from your struggle/addiction for the *next* 24 hours and you'll follow up with them tomorrow to let them know if you did.

Once you have done so, initial here: _____ Date: _____

>> **SCRIPTURE READING: 1 Corinthians 12**

DAY 73

The Richest I've Ever Been

Funds are low again, hallelujah! That means God trusts us and is willing to leave His reputation in our hands.

C. T. Studd

WHEN I WAS IN SEMINARY, I worked twenty hours a week for $10 an hour. That's as much as I could work while studying, writing papers, serving at church and in local ministries, and trying to date Laura. After I paid all my monthly bills, I had $2.50 per day left to save or spend. There was a grocery store chain that would drop off unsold expired bread for free at the seminary, so I would eat four slices of the bread and splurge on a small hot chocolate out of an old seventies vending machine for forty cents. Needless to say, I weighed twenty pounds less than I do now.

I slept on a twin mattress my brother had bought for me. It was on the cold concrete floor of a downtown Dallas flat that my friend Sam allowed me to live in because God had led him to invite me in as a roommate, rent- and bill-free. I wore old clothes and worn-out boots. I was broke.

But it's the richest I've ever been. And ever will be.

When my funds were few, my faith grew. God was it for me. He was my all, and He was my Provider, my Father. I needed Him for my actual daily bread. And in that daily desperation, He showed me that joy, contentment, peace, and every other thing is found in Him. My needs were met and my soul was fed. I've never been so content as when I had so little. And that's not because I was or am some super saint; it's because of the promise of God found in Philippians, written by a man who had much and was stripped of everything, including his freedom. Yet the refrain of Paul's prison letter to the church in Philippi is to rejoice.

So no matter what you have or don't have—whether you're experiencing material, relational, physical, or mental poverty—if you have God, you are rich, richer than the richest person alive. It's our goods that often keep us from our God. When we have much, we seem to have less need for God, though He is the one who gives us all. Truly, less is more. Even as I write this, I am wearing my favorite T-shirt, which serves as a reminder to me. It's a Shane & Shane shirt that reads this from Psalm 23: *I shall not want.*

This powerful promise that the secret of being content is found in Christ alone is from Philippians 4:11–13:

> Not that I am speaking of being in need, for I have learned in whatever situation I am to be content. I know how to be brought low, and I know how to abound. In any and every circumstance, I have learned the secret of facing plenty and hunger, abundance and need. I can do all things through him who strengthens me.

If you are in lack right now, you are actually in a great place (a much better place than if you were in a season of plenty), because God becomes greater the less we have. Write a prayer asking Him for the contentment that comes from Christ alone.

_____

_____

_____

_____

_____

In a position of humility, pray and ask God to keep you from your struggle for the next 24 hours.

Text or call a brother or sister in Christ to let them know if you've stayed free from your struggle for the *past* 24 hours. Tell them you're also committing, by God's strength, to staying free from your struggle/addiction for the *next* 24 hours and you'll follow up with them tomorrow to let them know if you did.

Once you have done so, initial here: ____ Date: _____

» SCRIPTURE READING: Galatians 4

DAY 74

Give God Your Worst

God seemed to have granted the greatest favors to the greatest sinners, as more signal monuments of His mercy.

Brother Lawrence

PEOPLE TALK ABOUT GIVING GOD your best, which is good to do. But I am a firm believer in giving God your worst, giving Him your trash.

I love art, and one of my favorite artists in the world is a social-commentary artist named Chris Jordan. He recreates renditions of famous masterpieces from various items. To make a commentary on the number of deaths caused by lung cancer, he constructed a massive mosaic of a skull, but upon looking closely, you'll find it's comprised of cigarette boxes. And when he wanted to depict the problem of plastics polluting our oceans, he collected bits of sea trash that washed up on the shore. Parts of flip-flops, LEGOs, bits of old tires, a toothbrush, and more were meticulously and purposefully organized to recreate the famous Japanese masterpiece *Under the Wave off Kanagawa*. From a distance, it just looks like a beautiful painting, but if you get close, you'll find it's made up of broken pieces fitted together.

God does this if you'll let Him. I gave Him the broken pieces of my life, my trash. And He took them. He didn't make them disappear. Instead, He redeemed them by repurposing them. He brought order to chaos and pieced together all my broken parts to make them into something for my good and His glory. Just before writing this entry, a man asked me what I did. I freely and easily told him that I work with addicts because I myself am a recovering alcoholic.

Redemption.

When people are going through hardship and have made terrible mistakes, I have empathy, because I remember my alcoholism and the regret I carried for years.

Redemption.

When people are walking down a path of sin, I can speak with authority that it's not what they want, because I know the loss of a decade exchanged for the fleeting, poisonous pleasure of sin.

Redemption.

So give God your trash. He'll repurpose, reengineer, and restore. He did it for me; He'll do it for you, if you'll let Him. Give Him your worst and watch Him work.

This powerful promise that God takes our mess and makes it a message is found in Romans 8:28 (and Eph. 1:11).

> And we know that for those who love God all things work together for good, for those who are called according to his purpose.

Write a prayer below giving God your worst mistakes and greatest sins. Turn them over to Him and ask Him to redeem your pain. He will.

In a position of humility, pray and ask God to keep you from your struggle for the next 24 hours.

Text or call a brother or sister in Christ to let them know if you've stayed free from your struggle for the *past* 24 hours. Tell them you're also committing, by God's strength, to staying free from your struggle/addiction for the *next* 24 hours and you'll follow up with them tomorrow to let them know if you did.

Once you have done so, initial here: _____ Date: _____

>> **SCRIPTURE READING: Psalm 23**

DAY 75

False Evidence Appearing Real

The fear of God is the death of every other fear; like a mighty lion, it chases all other fears before it.

Charles Spurgeon

FEAR IS A POWERFUL THING. Fear holds unwanted sway over our lives. Fear makes us doubt God, wrecks our relationships, and enslaves our minds, emotions, and decisions. Fear is a tool of Satan and a form of sick pagan worship that roots from the flesh. We are a frail and fearful race. We see things at face value, believing the worst will come and God will not intervene. In fact, FEAR is False Evidence Appearing Real. Fear causes us to hide rather than hope. Fear compels us to believe that God has forgotten us and then worry, fretfulness, stress, and ungodly reactions reign.

But God has said, "Do not fear." Interestingly and ironically, not only is it one of the most often repeated refrains of the Bible, but it is stated 365 times, once for every day, as if God knew we would be prone to fear daily. God is either sovereign and providential or He isn't. And He is. When we fear God, in the sense of reverence and yielding to God alone, there is nothing left to fear. Truly, nothing.

So don't believe the FEAR, the False Evidence Appearing Real, that makes you believe God has forgotten, He doesn't see your problems or pain, or He won't come through or deliver you. He will. Fear Him and no one or nothing else. He is God Most High, and He is your Father. In fact, the Bible promises that in Christ, He has given you power, love, and self-control as the antidotes to fear.

This powerful promise that fear is not from God and that He instead has given you power, love, and self-control is found in 2 Timothy 1:7.

> For God gave us a spirit not of fear but of power and love and self-control.

Write a prayer below asking God to fan into flame power, love, and self-control in you and that by His strength you would not give way to fear of anyone or anything but Him alone.

In a position of humility, pray and ask God to keep you from your struggle for the next 24 hours.

Text or call a brother or sister in Christ to let them know if you've stayed free from your struggle for the *past* 24 hours. Tell them you're also committing, by God's strength, to staying free from your struggle/addiction for the *next* 24 hours and you'll follow up with them tomorrow to let them know if you did.

Once you have done so, initial here: _____ Date: _____

>> **SCRIPTURE READING: 2 Timothy 1**

DAY 76

Bryan and Ethel

Knowing God is more than knowing about Him; it is a matter of dealing with Him as He opens up to you, and being dealt with by Him as He takes knowledge of you. Knowing about Him is a necessary precondition of trusting in Him, but the width of our knowledge about Him is no gauge of the depth of our knowledge of Him.

J. I. Packer

MY GOOD FRIEND FROM COLLEGE, Bryan, went off to medical school, and the intensity of studying didn't allow for much dating. He wasn't even looking for a woman, but there she was, and it seemed to him their time together would be inevitable. They didn't know each other, so as with any relationship, the first few times together were terribly awkward.

But the more time Bryan spent with Ethel, the more he felt like himself around her. They soon were spending hours together weekly, and he became enthralled with her. He wanted to know all about her and find out what made her tick. Physical touch became a normal thing, never inappropriate. Bryan would spend hours with Ethel and often find himself gazing in awe at her. But as the semester came to a close, the relationship abruptly ended without so much as a goodbye. And all along, the truth of the matter was that Bryan was in fact married to another girl—his college sweetheart, Heather.

You might wonder how I could so publicly write about my friend and his side relationship with Ethel.

Ethel was a cadaver, a body donated to medical science to teach my friend all about the human body.

We often treat God like Ethel. We spend time examining God. We are in God's presence but don't get to know Him, only about Him. We treat God like a cadaver as we dissect His Word, examining every facet and the intricacies therein. But just as Bryan knew all about Ethel while never knowing her, we can know all about God without knowing Him. The Pharisees were known for this. They memorized God's Word, followed God's laws, and even prayed and fasted, but they never knew God.

There are two words in biblical Greek for knowing: *ginosko* and *oida*. *Ginosko* is knowledge; *oida* is relationship. It doesn't matter if you know a lot about God; it matters if you know Him.

This powerful promise of eternal life from knowing (relationally knowing) God through Jesus is found in John 17:3.

> And this is eternal life, that they know you, the only true God, and Jesus Christ whom you have sent.

223

Write a prayer below asking God to help you know Him more. Confess the ways you know about God without knowing Him. Ask Him to deepen your relationship with Him by spending time in His Word, in prayer, and in worship with His people.

_____

_____

_____

_____

_____

In a position of humility, pray and ask God to keep you from your struggle for the next 24 hours.

Text or call a brother or sister in Christ to let them know if you've stayed free from your struggle for the *past* 24 hours. Tell them you're also committing, by God's strength, to staying free from your struggle/addiction for the *next* 24 hours and you'll follow up with them tomorrow to let them know if you did.

Once you have done so, initial here: ____ Date: _____

» SCRIPTURE READING: Psalm 84

DAY 77

Pleasures, Measures, and Treasures

Our body has this defect that, the more it is provided care and comforts, the more needs and desires it finds.

Teresa of Ávila

THE WORLD OFFERS YOU COMFORT, identity, and value in the form of pleasures, measures, and treasures. These are the ways we worship the created instead of the Creator, and our hearts are lured away from the Lover and Keeper of our souls. I am particularly given to pleasures and measures. I've always struggled with addiction and bingeing. I reasoned that if one of something was good, then twelve must be great, and it didn't matter whether it was cookies or glasses of Scotch. I loved the feeling of being sedated, no matter if it was alcohol, painkillers, or even cold medicine.

And then there are measures. I felt better about myself if I was better than you. And not in a holier-than-thou way but in a more-successful-than-thou way. I wanted to be the best, the most popular, or the hardest worker. Treasures weren't my drug of choice in the past, but that doesn't mean I am somehow immune for life. Everyone struggles with some form of those three sins and offerings of the world. But the life they give in the moment is ensnaring and lethal. An idol (what you worship) will give you what you want in the moment because it knows that what it gets is you in the end.

225

The way out of the trap is to find your pleasure, measure, and treasure in Christ. Allow Him to be your pleasure in life—whether you eat or drink or whatever you do, do it all to the glory of God (1 Cor. 10:31). Enjoy life with Him relationally and don't look for life in fleeting, addictive pleasures. Now, we aren't ascetics either, who seek to abstain from all pleasure, but instead we enjoy God's good creation while giving Him thanks. You measure yourself by Christ, realizing that you are a sinner saved by grace. You are an adopted son or daughter of the Father. And thus the only measure is to seek to become more like Christ by the working of the Spirit and the washing of the Word. And treasures, store up treasures in heaven by good works done unto God for others' good and His glory. You will be rewarded, but don't labor for that which moths and rust destroy.

The answer isn't to stay away from pleasures, measures, and treasures; the answer is to seek them in Christ alone, for in Him we live and move and have our being. Live for Him, and in Him you'll find all of life—life everlasting.

This powerful promise that whoever does the will of God abides forever is found in 1 John 2:15–17.

> Do not love the world or the things in the world. If anyone loves the world, the love of the Father is not in him. For all that is in the world—the desires of the flesh and the desires of the eyes and pride of life—is not from the Father but is from the world. And the world is passing away along with its desires, but whoever does the will of God abides forever.

Write a prayer below asking God to set your mind, body, and soul to rightly pursue pleasures, measures, and treasures in Him and not the world. Confess to Him which of these you struggle with and how/when.

_____

_____

_____

_____

_____

In a position of humility, pray and ask God to keep you from your struggle for the next 24 hours.

Text or call a brother or sister in Christ to let them know if you've stayed free from your struggle for the *past* 24 hours. Tell them you're also committing, by God's strength, to staying free from your struggle/addiction for the *next* 24 hours and you'll follow up with them tomorrow to let them know if you did.

Once you have done so, initial here: _____ Date: _____

≫ SCRIPTURE READING: 1 John 2

DAY 78

Weakness Works

Bibles read without prayer; sermons heard without prayer; marriages contracted without prayer; journeys undertaken without prayer; residences chosen without prayer; friendships formed without prayer; the daily act of prayer itself hurried over, or gone through without heart: these are the kind of downward steps by which many a Christian descends to a condition of spiritual palsy, or reaches the point where God allows them to have a tremendous fall.

J. C. Ryle

MY KIDS ARE KIND OF HELPLESS in most ways. They can't even open a simple granola bar wrapper. Incessantly throughout the day, Laura and I get a barrage of "Daddy, can you open this?" "Momma, can you get me that?" They can't reach things, make their own meals, brush their own teeth, read bedtime books, or give themselves baths. Just today, I was out grocery shopping with them and the clerk gave them each a lollipop. My son and daughter were twisting and pulling and biting at the wrapper without any success, and all they did was mess up a perfectly good treat.

I should be more like my kids: totally and unashamedly dependent on the Father. If I'm honest, I spend way too many of my days opening my own packages of opportunity, trying to clean myself of my sin by making things right or minimizing sin rather than seeking to be washed in confession and forgiveness; reading and applying (or not applying) Scripture without prayer; and doing what I think is best without asking for permission from my Father.

Fact of the matter is, my children in their weakness are in a much better position of humility and care than I am. My grown-up, can-do mentality is not a good thing. Even now, I'm realizing I've started writing today without stopping to pray first (so I'm pausing right now). Oh, the blessings, provision, help, wisdom, and lightened load I might experience if I would live with my Father as my children do theirs.

So whether it's an affliction, an inability, a struggle, loneliness, frustration, or fear, go to your Father. Don't be a stubborn child wrenching apart and wrecking a perfectly good lollipop. Hand everything over to your loving and all-present Father, and simply acknowledge your weakness, for when you are weak, He is strong.

This powerful promise that God's strength for you is made perfect in our weakness is found in 2 Corinthians 12:9.

> But he said to me, "My grace is sufficient for you, for my power is made perfect in weakness." Therefore I will boast all the more gladly of my weaknesses, so that the power of Christ may rest upon me.

Write a prayer below acknowledging how you have been proud or independent, and then with upward facing hands, release that to God and simply say, "Father, please help." He will.

_____

_____

_____

_____

_____

In a position of humility, pray and ask God to keep you from your struggle for the next 24 hours.

Text or call a brother or sister in Christ to let them know if you've stayed free from your struggle for the *past* 24 hours. Tell them you're also committing, by God's strength, to staying free from your struggle/addiction for the *next* 24 hours and you'll follow up with them tomorrow to let them know if you did.

Once you have done so, initial here: ____ Date: _____

≫ SCRIPTURE READING: 2 Corinthians 12

DAY 79

Driving in the Dark

It is sottish ignorance and infidelity to suppose that, under the gospel, there is no communication between God and us but what is, on His part, in laws, commands, and promises; and on ours, by obedience performed in our strength, and upon our convictions unto them. To exclude hence the real internal operations of the Holy Ghost, is to destroy the gospel.

John Owen

WHEN ALL THREE OF OUR YOUNG KIDS sleep at the same time, it is an alignment of the planets, and all is well in the world. The chaos turned to peace is nothing short of a miracle. So this past summer when we were on a road trip and all three fell asleep, the GPS on my phone had to be on silent. Laura would tell you I'm horrible with directions, and what little directional ability I had has atrophied since the advent of maps on smartphones.

While we were driving with all three asleep and the volume down on the GPS, my attention to the map went up. I didn't trust myself, so I glanced incessantly at my phone to make sure I was not missing a turn or going to hit some pocket of traffic. And Laura, who was obviously going to the same place I was, of course was helping me look for signs and turns (not because I'm a bad driver, though, right?).

This is how we must go through life. We have the Word of God, the Spirit of God, and the people of God to help us navigate. We are driving in the darkness of this world, and with the thousands of daily decisions we face, it's vital that we glance down to the Word and up to the Lord as our directional guides. If you aren't doing this, and are just waiting for an audible voice or a burning bush, you may be waiting a long, long time. The Lord has promised He will guide us with the living, active Word that is a lamp unto our feet and the living, active Spirit Who leads us on our journey Home.

Like me driving with a silent GPS, be sure to keep glancing down to the Word and up to the Lord, always talking with the other believers who are headed toward the same destination. You'll get where you're going, for He is faithful.

This powerful promise of God that the Spirit will lead you is found in Romans 8:14.

For all who are led by the Spirit of God are sons of God.

Write a prayer below asking God to help you faithfully turn to the Bible and use it as your guide. Also look up to the Lord and thank him for his love and direction.

_____

_____

_____

_____

_____

In a position of humility, pray and ask God to keep you from your struggle for the next 24 hours.

Text or call a brother or sister in Christ to let them know if you've stayed free from your struggle for the *past* 24 hours. Tell them you're also committing, by God's strength, to staying free from your struggle/addiction for the *next* 24 hours

and you'll follow up with them tomorrow to let them know if you did.

Once you have done so, initial here: _____ Date: _____

>> **SCRIPTURE READING: Isaiah 53**

DAY 80

Deistic and Theistic Fear

The knowledge of God is very far from the love of Him.
Blaise Pascal

WE DIDN'T HAVE DRINKABLE WATER where I lived in Haiti, but there was a spigot in the local cemetery that always had running water. So we would load up in this huge, rickety lorry with a chateau dlo (which you might remember from Day 18 is a massive plastic water tank, literally "water house") and head down to the cemetery in the dead of night (pun unavoidably intended). I have no idea why Pastor Henri waited till nightfall to get water from the cemetery, but that was our offense. The first time we did this, I felt like I was in a zombie apocalypse movie, which was only emphasized by the fact that zombie lore originated in Haiti (nice).

Many Haitian cemeteries have above-ground mausoleums and little house-like structures built above graves. This may just be a French thing, as it looked like the cemeteries in New

Orleans, except that people were both hanging out and living in these structures. And our creaky, old truck alerted all the grave dwellers that we were there. We stopped the truck, they filled five-gallon buckets from the graveyard with water from the spigot, and my job was to lift the buckets into the truck, dump the water into the chateau dlo, and pass the empties back. It was a half-hour ordeal.

On our first water run, I couldn't help but notice that as I emptied the buckets one by one, a voodoo priest (I think, I didn't ask for his business card) was chanting and lighting fires around us and the truck. Which meant I was in the middle of a burning pentagram in a graveyard (awesome).

"Hey, Pastor Henri," I said, buckets sloshing, "umm, there's a man lighting fires around us."

Without hesitation in his speech or passing of the buckets, he said, "Bon" (which is like "oh" or "well" in Kreyòl, meaning "good"). "Greater is He that is in you than he that is in the world."

In that moment, I realized I *knew* that Scripture, but he *believed* it. I had a deistic fear. I knew God existed, but He wasn't going to intervene and help me, so I needed to help myself in that moment. Pastor Henri had a theistic fear and believed God existed. Pastor Henri understood God was sovereign and providentially in control, and in fearing God, he had nothing and no one left to fear except God alone.

We finished loading the water and drove right over the worthless pentagram of fire and the curse without cause that wouldn't light (Prov. 26:2).

In Christ, you have nothing and no one left to fear. Fear God alone and be free. Fear no evil—no supernatural evil; no physical evil; no evil man or woman; not Satan, or his demons; not physical affliction, nor years of addiction or struggle. God is over all and dwells within you by the Holy Spirit. And in that, His perfect love drives out fear.

233

This powerful promise that God is in you and that He is greater than he, Satan, who is in the world, is found in 1 John 4:4.

> Little children, you are from God and have overcome them, for he who is in you is greater than he who is in the world.

Write a prayer below asking God for the faith and power to believe that He is in you, and that as a result, there is nothing and no one left to fear but Him alone.

_____

_____

_____

_____

_____

In a position of humility, pray and ask God to keep you from your struggle for the next 24 hours.

Text or call a brother or sister in Christ to let them know if you've stayed free from your struggle for the *past* 24 hours. Tell them you're also committing, by God's strength, to staying free from your struggle/addiction for the *next* 24 hours and you'll follow up with them tomorrow to let them know if you did.

Once you have done so, initial here: _____ Date: _____

>> SCRIPTURE READING: 1 John 4

DAY 81

No Shame from Pain

Shame is a thing to shame only those who want to appear, not those who want to be. Shame is to shame those who want to pass their examination, not those who would get into the heart of things.

George MacDonald

ONE OF THE FIRST MEN to disciple me, Chad Hampsch, taught me that, apart from the redemption of Christ, men use love to get sex and women use sex to get love. It's a sinful cycle that gives each gender what they want in the moment and leaves them with a greater void afterward.

There was a woman who was used by men for sex. And truth be told, she was likely using men for their provision and affection. Burning through relationship after relationship was devouring her life. And after multiple failed attempts at a relationship, there she was with yet another man, broken-hearted and searching for true love.

She met a man over a drink one afternoon, and her life would never be the same. She was gathering water and a man asked her for a drink. That man, unbeknownst to her, was Jesus. She said she was surprised He would ask a woman like her for a drink, and He in turn offered her living water so that she would never thirst again. In John 4, she asked for the water He offered, and first He said, "Go, call your husband, and come here." She said, "I have no husband." He replied, "You are right in saying, 'I have no husband'; for you have had five husbands, and the one you now have is not your husband" (vv. 16–18). In His revealing He knew her entire

235

history of broken, sinful relationships, she realized she was not talking to a mere mortal.

But Jesus didn't say this to shame her; He acknowledged her sin so that she could be free. For truly, no one knows they need a savior apart from knowing they have sin. He was inviting her into a life of forgiveness and healing.

Maybe that's your situation right now. You've picked up this book in private because you've had multiple lovers, but the truth is, your lovers have you. Lovers of porn, pills, gambling highs, disordered eating, relationship addiction, or whatever you're attached to. Jesus is extending you living water, that you might never thirst for the poisonous affections of this world again. You need not be ashamed of your struggles. Jesus not only knows them fully, but He loves you fully and longs to set you free. Shame is a tool of Satan to keep you in hiding. God has come to you in the midst of your struggle to free you.

And so it is true: in Christ alone, if you know pain, under His unquenchable grace, there is no shame. That woman is known throughout history as the woman at the well, *not* the woman of six men. Her identity was in Christ, and she went on to lead her town to Christ as well by telling them openly about Jesus, Who knew her shame and loved her all the same. Don't let shame keep you from Christ or from sharing your story of redemption.

This powerful promise that there is no one, no person, no demon, or even Satan who can accuse or shame God's children is found in Romans 8:31–34:

> What then shall we say to these things? If God is for us, who can be against us? He who did not spare his own Son but gave him up for us all, how will he not also with him graciously give us all things? Who shall bring any charge against God's elect? It is God who justifies. Who is to condemn? Christ Jesus

is the one who died—more than that, who was raised—who is at the right hand of God, who indeed is interceding for us.

Write a prayer below giving God every bit of the shame of your past and present, and pray back the promise above, thanking Him that in Christ no one can bring a charge or condemnation against you.

_____

_____

_____

_____

_____

In a position of humility, pray and ask God to keep you from your struggle for the next 24 hours.

Text or call a brother or sister in Christ to let them know if you've stayed free from your struggle for the *past* 24 hours. Tell them you're also committing, by God's strength, to staying free from your struggle/addiction for the *next* 24 hours and you'll follow up with them tomorrow to let them know if you did.

Once you have done so, initial here: _____ Date: _____

›› SCRIPTURE READING: John 4

DAY 82

Foreign Frequencies

There is nothing morbid about the confession of sins, so long as we go on to give thanks for the forgiveness of sins. It is fine to look inwards, so long as it leads us immediately to look outwards and upwards again.

John R. W. Stott

WE WERE DRIVING BACK from visiting my dear grandpa-in-law, Da, at his home in Weatherford. The kids were watching a movie in my wife's car. We tune the radio to the frequency of the DVD player, and the movie's audio plays through the car speakers. So there we were, cruising down the highway listening to Curious George or some innocuous kid show. With my precious wife beside me and my treasured children in the back seat, I started randomly thinking about drinking. I was daydreaming about what it would be like if I weren't married, had no kids, and was sitting on a patio about five drinks into the afternoon. It was a sunny Sunday, one of the first of spring, and that was always the perfect time for day drinking. I was lost in my thoughts about how carefree life would be—no diapers to change, no chicken nuggets to heat up, not a care in the world, just an afternoon buzz and some good music.

But here is why those thoughts about drinking began. Without my even realizing it, we had driven into a town. In that town was a radio station with a stronger signal than the DVD player. And without even perceiving it, the frequency changed from a children's story to a song, and in turn also my mind from thoughts of a mischievous monkey to a day of getting drunk. The song made me nostalgically reminisce about my drinking days.

After about five minutes, I switched off the radio, turned to Laura, and said, "I need you to know, I've been daydreaming about drinking and how great it would be to just be alone, drunk on a patio, all by myself." And with that, the frequency changed again. Immediately, my God-fearing wife reminded me that those days were death, that God had redeemed my life, that the foreign frequency I was hearing was no song, but a lullaby of death, lulling my soul to sin. I confessed. She spoke truth and prayed. The lies fled. And I was free.

Beware of the foreign frequencies. They'll creep into your mind and be a siren song to lure you to death. Run to the light, listen to truth, and head Home.

This powerful promise that when we bring sin into the light, it dies and Christ shines on us is found in Ephesians 5:11–17.

> Take no part in the unfruitful works of darkness, but instead expose them. For it is shameful even to speak of the things that they do in secret. But when anything is exposed by the light, it becomes visible, for anything that becomes visible is light. Therefore it says,
>
> > "Awake, O sleeper,
> >   and arise from the dead,
> > and Christ will shine on you."
>
> Look carefully then how you walk, not as unwise but as wise, making the best use of the time, because the days are evil. Therefore do not be foolish, but understand what the will of the Lord is.

Write a prayer below asking God to tune your heart to Him, to help you know when a foreign frequency has entered your mind, and to have the courage to confess it to a brother or sister in Christ.

_____

_____

_____

_____

_____

In a position of humility, pray and ask God to keep you from your struggle for the next 24 hours.

Text or call a brother or sister in Christ to let them know if you've stayed free from your struggle for the *past* 24 hours. Tell them you're also committing, by God's strength, to staying free from your struggle/addiction for the *next* 24 hours and you'll follow up with them the next day to let them know if you did.

Once you have done so, initial here: _____ Date: _____

>> **SCRIPTURE READING: Ephesians 6**

DAY 83

Escape Room

Instead of asking yourself whether you believe or not, ask yourself whether you have, this day, done one thing because he said, Do it, or once abstained because he said, Do not do it. It is simply absurd to say you believe, or even want to believe in him, if you do not do anything he tells you.

George MacDonald

I'VE ONLY DONE ONE ESCAPE ROOM (not counting the two times I've been inside an IKEA). It was a team outing with our recovery ministry. We signed our waivers, were locked inside from the outside, and then the confusion, fun, and adrenaline began, all while some random dude watched our every move on closed-circuit cameras.

It was exhilarating to solve a puzzle and advance to the next clue, leading us further through the adventure. And even though there was an eeriness to the place, it was fun-filled. The payoff was instant when we cracked a code and advanced, and we didn't want to give up until we made it to the end. After a while, though, the fun wore off. We got frustrated. We wanted to ask the guy watching us on closed-circuit TVs for a hint. We had been in there almost two hours, and that was long enough.

Everyone wants out; no one wants to stay in an escape room. Unless, of course, you're human. Let me explain.

The Bible lays out similar imagery but says the escape room we are in is filled with things that pull at and toy with our affections. We are in the rooms of the world, but instead of trying to get out, we get comfortable and settle in. We like the surroundings, the pleasures, the offerings, the earnings. And all the while, we, too, have someone watching—whether we acknowledge Him or not. He wants us to escape. He wants to help us get out. He longs for our release from what has clouded our judgment and confused reality of the spiritual experience we are in. Temptation bids us to stay, sin a little, enjoy this room. But God whispers into our hearts, "There is a way out. Take it now."

The choice is then ours. Do we listen to God and escape with the path He's illumined? Or do we shun and scorn His voice by ignoring the Spirit's promptings and instead stay longer in the dark room of the world?

God has promised that no matter what room of temptation you find yourself in, He will always give you a way out.

This powerful promise that God will always give you a way of escape from every temptation is found in 1 Corinthians 10:13.

> No temptation has overtaken you that is not common to man. God is faithful, and he will not let you be tempted beyond your ability, but with the temptation he will also provide the way of escape, that you may be able to endure it.

Write a prayer below asking God to give you the awareness of His way out of temptation when it comes and the conviction to take it.

_____

_____

_____

_____

In a position of humility, pray and ask God to keep you from your struggle for the next 24 hours.

Text or call a brother or sister in Christ to let them know if you've stayed free from your struggle for the *past* 24 hours. Tell them you're also committing, by God's strength, to staying free from your struggle/addiction for the *next* 24 hours

and you'll follow up with them tomorrow to let them know if you did.

Once you have done so, initial here: _____ Date: _____

» **SCRIPTURE READING: 1 Corinthians 10**

DAY 84

The Surprising Gift within a Forest Fire

We can stand affliction better than we can prosperity, for in prosperity we forget God.

D. L. Moody

THE LODGEPOLE PINE HAS SEEDS. But those seeds will never come to be massive, mature trees without one thing. In addition to sunshine, water, and soil, the seeds of the lodgepole pine must have fire, a consuming fire, in order to bring forth life and reproduce. The pinecones of the lodgepole are covered by a resin that seals them off, and they will never break forth without a forest fire.

Additionally, within a forest is a great amount of undergrowth. The undergrowth is living, but it is not entirely beneficial to the forest. Instead, the underbrush actually consumes much of the water and nutrients that otherwise would be delivered to the towering trees. In a way, they are competing for the lifegiving resources of the forest.

Thus, a fire can be beneficial to a forest. The undergrowth is consumed and scorched from the earth, and the seeds of some pyrophytic trees that would otherwise remain unable to give new growth are released. Life from death; life that was stuck as potential because of prosperity. So it is also with afflictions, trials, and persecution in the Christian life. We often need the very thing we strive to avoid. I can attest to this.

I've told my community group that I have a strange and sobering yearning for a season of affliction. Why? Why in the world would I have an odd longing for hardship? It's not because I'm some sick, twisted person who enjoys pain. It's because I know that any time I go through a spiritual forest fire, the competing undergrowth of fear of man, people pleasing, idle time, idol time, pride, self-sufficiency, prayerlessness, self-actualizing activity, and squandering of time and money get scorched out of my life. The closest I've ever been to God, the most dependent I've ever been on Him, the freest I've ever been from the concerns of this world, have always been in the midst of hardship.

It's because, in the blaze of suffering, a strange promise of God comes to bear. Life breaks forth—life that could come only through the furnace of affliction. New seeds of spirituality are released, and new growth comes forth. And that is the gift of a forest fire. Don't go looking for one or set out to be a spiritual arsonist. That doesn't honor God. But when the affliction and suffering come, and Jesus promised us they would (John 16:33), remember God's promise: He will bring forth life, He will not waste your pain, and you will be more fruitful and mature in Christ as a result.

This powerful promise that suffering and affliction will result in character, endurance, hope, and maturity in Christ and in your faith is found in 1 Pet. 1:6–9 (see also Rom. 5:3–5).

In this you rejoice, though now for a little while, if necessary, you have been grieved by various trials, so that the tested genuineness of your faith—more precious than gold that perishes though it is tested by fire—may be found to result in praise and glory and honor at the revelation of Jesus Christ. Though you have not seen him, you love him. Though you do not now see him, you believe in him and rejoice with joy that is inexpressible and filled with glory, obtaining the outcome of your faith, the salvation of your souls.

Write a prayer below thanking God that in the midst of whatever suffering may befall you, He knows about it, He will walk through it with you, and you will come out closer to Him and more like Christ.

_____

_____

_____

_____

In a position of humility, pray and ask God to keep you from your struggle for the next 24 hours.

Text or call a brother or sister in Christ to let them know if you've stayed free from your struggle for the *past* 24 hours. Tell them you're also committing, by God's strength, to staying free from your struggle/addiction for the *next* 24 hours and you'll follow up with them tomorrow to let them know if you did.

Once you have done so, initial here: ____ Date: _____

≫ SCRIPTURE READING: John 16

DAY 85

Keep the Buzz Going

Apart from God every activity is merely a passing whiff of insignificance.
Alfred North Whitehead

IN MY LATE TWENTIES, I had a black coffee mug. It had to be black. I needed it to be black. Because if it was white, people would have noticed that it had Scotch in it. And drinking in the morning tends to give away the fact that you have a drinking problem. Why Scotch on a Saturday morning? Because it would keep the buzz going and the hangover at bay. I was a mess. And if I stopped drinking, pain would come and pleasure would end. It was simple logic and physiological reward: keep drinking.

So it may seem a little ironic that when I'm talking to people, especially alcoholics and addicts, about God, I tell them to keep sipping.

The Bible tells us not to get drunk with wine, which leads to debauchery—excessive indulgence in sensual pleasures— but instead to be filled with the Spirit. I see it like this: When I used to drink, I would say things I normally wouldn't say, do things I normally wouldn't do, and become a version of myself I normally wasn't. None of those were improvements; I became foul-mouthed and totally reckless.

Similar to how I was under the influence of alcohol, the Bible tells me to conversely be under the influence of the Spirit. And if I am, I will say things I normally wouldn't say, do things I normally wouldn't do, and become a version of myself I normally am not. And things done by the influence

246

of the Spirit are full of righteousness instead of regret. My daily default setting is the flesh—fleshly thoughts, desires, and actions. But if I am filled with the Spirit, meaning I give myself over to Him to be under His influence, I'll do more of what He does and less of what my fleshly self would do. So, it's good to be under the influence. Just make sure the influence you're under is the Spirit, not spirits.

You do this by sipping throughout the day. Quiet times are good, but they're entirely insufficient. You must sip throughout the day with prayer, worship music, Scripture, talking/texting with other believers, and acting in obedience. All that keeps you under the influence of the Spirit and out of your black mug.

This transformational truth that being under the influence of the Spirit keeps us from the flesh is found in Ephesians 5:18–20.

> And do not get drunk with wine, for that is debauchery, but be filled with the Spirit, addressing one another in psalms and hymns and spiritual songs, singing and making melody to the Lord with your heart, giving thanks always and for everything to God the Father in the name of our Lord Jesus Christ.

Write a prayer below giving yourself to the Holy Spirit's influence today. Yield to Him.

In a position of humility, pray and ask God to keep you from your struggle for the next 24 hours.

Text or call a brother or sister in Christ to let them know if you've stayed free from your struggle for the *past* 24 hours. Tell them you're also committing, by God's strength, to staying free from your struggle/addiction for the *next* 24 hours and you'll follow up with them tomorrow to let them know if you did.

Once you have done so, initial here: _____ Date: _____

>> **SCRIPTURE READING: Titus 3**

DAY 86

Pressures for Peace

As the Christian prays, he actually anticipates his own liberation from anxiety even when engulfed by it. Praying to God, he can no longer have it, nor be possessed by it.

Karl Barth

REMEMBER CHRIS JORDAN, the artist who creates masterpieces with trash that parallel how God redeems our past? Well, God also redeems our present trash. When I was growing up, I remember collecting aluminum cans with the kids across the street. It was the craziest thing. We would pick up trash, put it into a bag, and they exchanged it for money. I had no concept of such a thing. I couldn't believe those worthless cans could yield something valuable. I remember helping and seeing the massive black trash bag that became incrementally heavier, but I don't recall ever getting a cent (the neighbor kids kept the cash). But what I did get was a lifelong lesson.

God does this. He promises. He tells His children—you—to bring Him your weighty trash. Bring Him your accumulation of burdens, your worries, that you can no longer carry and were never designed to. What kind of God takes the weight we aren't even supposed to carry? Our God. The God of the Bible, and only Him. He takes the weight of worry, pressures, and fear and, get this, exchanges them for something of infinitely greater value. He, the Lord, takes our pressures and gives us peace. But there's a catch. Just like we kids had to take the cans to the metal exchange, you have to take your pressures to God.

And it's not just any peace He gives you. It's otherworldly. It's a supernatural, inexplicable peace. It's the kind of peace that makes doctors in cancer wards scratch their heads. In Christ, we are a wonder to this world, that despite our pressures and problems, we have peace. When the world frets, we are free. So, gather your trashed-out worries and woes. Take them to the feet of the Father with thanksgiving and receive your inexplicable exchange—the peace of Jesus Christ.

This powerful promise that God will take your pressures and give you the peace of Christ is found in Philippians 4:6–7.

> Do not be anxious about anything, but in everything by prayer and supplication with thanksgiving let your requests be made known to God. And the peace of God, which surpasses all understanding, will guard your hearts and your minds in Christ Jesus.

Write a prayer below taking all your worries and pressures to God. Explain them honestly and openly, and ask him to bless you with the peace of Christ.

_____

_____

_____

_____

_____

In a position of humility, pray and ask God to keep you from your struggle for the next 24 hours.

Text or call a brother or sister in Christ to let them know if you've stayed free from your struggle for the *past* 24 hours. Tell them you're also committing, by God's strength, to staying free from your struggle/addiction for the *next* 24 hours and you'll follow up with them tomorrow to let them know if you did.

Once you have done so, initial here: ____Date: _____

>> **SCRIPTURE READING: 1 Thessalonians 5**

DAY 87

Pick a List, Pick a Life

It does not spoil your happiness to confess your sin. The unhappiness is in not making the confession.

Charles Spurgeon

I WANT YOU to read through both lists below. Really read through them. Don't just glance over them.

LIST 1:	LIST 2:
• Division within God's family	• An aspect of worship
• Weariness	• Life and glory to God
• Sickness	• Burdens relieved
• Heaviness	• Forgiveness
• Separation from God	• Exaltation and justification
• Blocked communication with God	• Cleansing
• Further compounds sin	• Reconciliation with man
• Humbling/discipline from God	• Healing
	• Restoration with God
	• Warns others of danger
	• Freedom and mercy

Now I want you to write here which list you would want if you had to choose one: LIST # _____.

Are you sure? Will you do whatever it takes to live List 2 and not List 1?

Then confess your sin—to God and others. List 1 is what the Bible says you can expect with unconfessed sin. List 2 is what the Bible says you will get when you confess sin. And you have to choose one; in fact, you choose a list daily.

No one in their right mind would ever choose List 1, yet we live the reality that leads us to List 1 by not confessing sin daily to God and others.

No wonder we struggle and limp through life. Like most worthwhile things in life, confessing sin won't be easy, but it'll be good. So read those lists again. And decide to change. List 2 has transformed my life. I am free. I am fully known and fully loved. My walk with God is healthy, and my relationships are deeper and more rewarding than ever before. Go figure. If God says something is good, we can trust Him, no matter how hard it may be. Confessing sin is never easy—never. But

251

it's always good—always. Confess your sin to God (1 John 1:9) and another believer today (James 5:16).

This powerful promise that confession of sin leads to mercy and progression in life is found in Proverbs 28:13.

> Whoever conceals his transgressions will not prosper,
>   but he who confesses and forsakes them will obtain
>   mercy.

Write a prayer below confessing your sin to God and asking Him for the boldness and humility to confess it to another believer too.

_____

_____

_____

_____

_____

In a position of humility, pray and ask God to keep you from your struggle for the next 24 hours.

Text or call a brother or sister in Christ to let them know if you've stayed free from your struggle for the *past* 24 hours. Tell them you're also committing, by God's strength, to staying free from your struggle/addiction for the *next* 24 hours and you'll follow up with them tomorrow to let them know if you did.

Once you have done so, initial here: _____ Date: _____

≫ SCRIPTURE READING: Proverbs 28

DAY 88

The Fast Way to Kill Sin

Fasting helps express, deepens, confirms the resolution that we are ready to sacrifice anything, even ourselves, to attain what we seek for the kingdom of God.

Andrew Murray

GOD HAS MADE US body, mind, and soul. We are intertwined in these few short, fleeting years as humans with bodies that crave and minds given to be enslaved, and our immortal souls hang in the balance while steering through this world riddled with temptation and limitless daily choices.

Ascetics try to eliminate pleasure in an attempt to reach godliness. But God didn't design us to eliminate pleasure. He designed us to enjoy it (1 Tim. 6:17). He gave us the physical sense of warmth and touch. He gave us taste buds with zones of the tongue to enjoy the variety He placed on the earth. He gave us eyes and minds wired to notice and appreciate beauty. He gave us ears that detect melody and musical wonder. He gave us the sense of smell to realize and savor the sweetness or even the subtle scent of rain. But He did this so we would worship Him by enjoying His creation (Rom. 1:20). Instead, we worship His creation by enjoying it and neglect Him entirely.

Why the discussion of avoiding pleasures and all our senses when speaking of the fast way to kill sin? Because sin finds its allure in senses. Sin reaches us through our senses and then dulls us to the Creator as we worship the created. I have found personally and read throughout the Scriptures that when people are in sin, they fast, meaning they abstain from creature comforts, most often food itself. And in doing so, they find the fast way to kill sin.

When you fast from food, it's not so much that you have more time to pray during mealtime, though you will. It's that your spirit within is quickened and awakened. Spiritual calluses are cut away as you fast and seek God over the flesh. When you remove food, your body weakens, but your spirit is strengthened. And your resolve to resist temptation is increased. The more you feed the flesh, the easier it is to give in to temptation because you've trained your body and mind, "You crave, you get." The more you subdue the flesh ("You crave, but by God's strength you will not get"), the easier it is to resist temptation (1 Cor. 9:27). Spiritual acuity and alertness come. You will find that as you yield to the Spirit and not worldly comforts, namely food, you'll have increased spiritual vitality and feel emboldened in your soul. And by saying yes to the Spirit and not the daily special, you'll find it is, in a doubly true way, the fast way to kill sin.

Moses, David, Daniel, Esther, and countless other heroes of the faith fasted from food in times of seeking God, trials, acknowledgment of sin, and affliction. The Author and Perfector of our faith, God in flesh, fasted from food when He went into the wilderness and was tempted. Thus, when we find ourselves in a time of temptation, we would be wise to follow our Savior, fast, and wait on the faithfulness of God.

This powerful example of fasting and resisting temptation is found in Matthew 4:1–4.

> Then Jesus was led up by the Spirit into the wilderness to be tempted by the devil. And after fasting forty days and forty nights, he was hungry. And the tempter came and said to him, "If you are the Son of God, command these stones to become loaves of bread." But he answered, "It is written,

> "'Man shall not live by bread alone,
>   but by every word that comes from the mouth
>   of God.'"

Write a prayer below asking God to help you get free from sin as you fast today (or another day of your choosing). Watch and see if your spiritual resolve is strengthened against the taunts of temptation.

MEDICAL NOTE: If you have any concerns or preexisting conditions that could make fasting unsafe, please consult a medical professional. A physical limitation that prevents fasting in no way makes you less spiritual, nor will it stand in Christ's way of victory over sin in your life.

_____

_____

_____

_____

_____

In a position of humility, pray and ask God to keep you from your struggle for the next 24 hours.

Text or call a brother or sister in Christ to let them know if you've stayed free from your struggle for the *past* 24 hours. Tell them you're also committing, by God's strength, to staying free from your struggle/addiction for the *next* 24 hours and you'll follow up with them tomorrow to let them know if you did.

Once you have done so, initial here: _____ Date: _____

>> **SCRIPTURE READING: Mark 9**

DAY 89

Deep Sharing = Deep Fellowship

The Church is the place where we learn not how self-sufficient we are, but where we learn what sin really is. The Church is the place where the Pharisee learns to say with the Publican: Lord, have mercy on me, a sinner.

Sir Edwyn C. Hoskyns

MY COMMUNITY GROUP GUYS, Mike and Shane, know everything about me. Everything—past and present. They know my ditches, my sin struggles, my temptations, my ugly thoughts, my critical spirit. You'd think since they are aware of all the bad things about me, they'd keep their distance. The exact opposite is true. We have a deep, deep bond because of the honesty and depth of confession in our relationship. We meet weekly and discuss three things: (1) How have we fed our souls (abiding/prayer/Word/worship)? (2) How have we fed our flesh (sin/temptation/thought life)? (3) How have we fed others? (discipleship/evangelism/giving/serving).

This is a crazy truism from Scripture, a promise (and you'll find it to be as well): only in Christ, when you are fully known, will you be fully loved. The world says put your resume, all your best, forward, and then you'll be loved. In Christ, the Lord says be humble and honest about your weaknesses and then you'll have deep fellowship, not shallow or worldly friends.

And remember that no matter what deep, dark, and ugly thing you're honest about, the blood of Christ cleanses you from all sin.

The promise from God for fellowship is found in 1 John 1:7:

But if we walk in the light, as he is in the light, we have fellowship with one another, and the blood of Jesus his Son cleanses us from all sin.

Write a prayer below asking God to give you the courage to truly bare your soul with a trusted brother or sister in Christ so that you may be fully known and fully loved and have true fellowship with one another.

_____

_____

_____

_____

_____

In a position of humility, pray and ask God to keep you from your struggle for the next 24 hours.

Text or call a brother or sister in Christ to let them know if you've stayed free from your struggle for the *past* 24 hours. Tell them you're also committing, by God's strength, to staying free from your struggle/addiction for the *next* 24 hours and you'll follow up with them tomorrow to let them know if you did.

Once you have done so, initial here: ____ Date: _____

≫ SCRIPTURE READING: 1 John 1

DAY 90

Given For

If Jesus Christ be God and died for me, then no sacrifice can be too great for me to make for Him.

C. T. Studd

I WAS ABLE TO GET THROUGH high school without studying because I could recall what was said in the classroom. But college exams were a different story, compounded by binge drinking and sleeping through class. Shocker.

I failed an accounting class, which was not only a personal failure but also a huge waste of my parents' money. It was the first thing I can remember not being able to achieve by just winging it or natural ability, and it stung. The reality of failure hit me hard. I don't exactly remember the thought progression, but I found myself walking home knowing exactly what I was going to do.

I went up into my room, got my hunting knife, and drove out to a secluded lakeshore. I sat on a piece of driftwood and began dragging that knife across my left forearm. I couldn't have put words to it at the time, but it was because of the pain within. The internal pain was too great. I wasn't walking with God and had no way to cope. So, in my brokenness, the way to deal with the pain of failure was to create a greater pain or perhaps a release through external pain. Or, in the moment, maybe it was a confused way of trying to self-punish for the foolishness. But a person can't pay for his own sins with his own blood, and cutting doesn't resolve anything. In fact, Scripture time and time again correlates cutting to the evil realm and demon worship.

But something happened on that shore of Lake Waco. I pulled out my journal and began drawing. I knew beforehand that I was going to hurt myself, but didn't have a plan to draw. I drew Jesus on the cross. And across the top, with the cross splitting the two words, wrote: *Given For*. And then farther below: *For Given*.

Even in my self-destruction, self-loathing, self-harm, and self-absorption, God was calling to me and reminding me. *This*, all my sin, is what Jesus was GIVEN FOR. He was given for forgiveness. Period. There's no other way or name by which people are saved (Acts 4:12). Jesus: given for and thus we are forgiven.

He was there with me in that moment. And He's there with you now. He's not mad at you; He loves you and longs to save you. He wants to take your pain. Whether you cope by cutting, pride, self-righteousness, food, drink, sex, or drugs, there is a better choice than your drug of choice: Jesus. He *promises* rest for your soul in Matthew 11:28–30.

> Come to me, all who labor and are heavy laden, and I will give you rest. Take my yoke upon you, and learn from me, for I am gentle and lowly in heart, and you will find rest for your souls. For my yoke is easy, and my burden is light.

Write a prayer below confessing the ways you try to find rest for your soul outside of Jesus, then ask Him today to give your soul rest.

In a position of humility, pray and ask God to keep you from your struggle for the next 24 hours.

Text or call a brother or sister in Christ to let them know if you've stayed free from your struggle for the *past* 24 hours. Tell them you're also committing, by God's strength, to staying free from your struggle/addiction for the *next* 24 hours and you'll follow up with them tomorrow to let them know if you did.

Once you have done so, initial here: _____ Date: _____

>> SCRIPTURE READING: Matthew 11

Conclusion

CONGRATULATIONS! But not for completing ninety days; congrats on doing Day 90. And you've done it for ninety days in a row. That's no small thing.

Your journey is underway, but it isn't done; it's only just begun. Don't worry that the book is over. It was never about the book. It was about learning to surrender daily, repent daily, confess daily to another, and depend on God (along with others in the body of Christ) daily to fight your battles against sin. So put the book down, but don't ever put down the disciplines and promises of God you've learned these last ninety days. In them lies the key to a radical, transformed, full, abundant life in Christ, focused on your Savior and not on your sin.

He loves you. He carries you daily. He will never leave nor forsake you. And He has a wild, wonderful life ahead for you—free from the hangover of pain and remorse that always follows sin's fleeting, poisonous pleasure.

Others out there need to know hope. No one needs a Savior apart from sin, and everyone has sin—it's the common denominator of humankind. So tell those you meet about the transforming love and power of Christ. God has saved you to send you. You are now His ambassador and minister of reconciliation, and you can bring other sinners to the loving hands of Christ. Tell your neighbors, your coworkers, your roommates, your family, your pastor . . . tell everyone how Jesus has freed you.

As you read at the beginning, if you fall, fall forward, kneeling in confession of sin, kneeling in asking God to give you freedom one day at a time, kneeling in surrender to your Master, kneeling in humble thanksgiving. This isn't about sobriety; it's a daily walk with your God, and He will bring sobriety and so much more. Be certain that He isn't mad at you, He loves you, and He longs to walk with you one day at a time.

Surely you have been won by the Lord Jesus Christ. And this battle on this side of eternity as we walk Home will be won one day at a time. As Paul wrote to the Galatians,

> Walk by the Spirit, and you will not gratify the desires of the flesh. (Gal. 5:16)

> For freedom Christ has set us free; stand firm therefore, and do not submit again to a yoke of slavery. (Gal. 5:1)

So, kneel or raise your arms to heaven in dedication and praise to the Lord Jesus Christ who lives to set the captives free.

You might be wondering, *Well, I've been asking the Spirit to help me war against a particular sin through this book. Do I now have to reread it for the next sin I'm aware of?* No. The book didn't bring you freedom; Christ did. Just keep that daily surrender and daily proactive commitment with another person intact, and make war!

And just in case any part of you is thinking your past will hinder God from using or blessing you in the future, allow me to tell you about my friend David. He became addicted to painkillers in high school, which progressed to a heroin addiction. After more than a decade of using, he confessed to his wife and went through detox and recovery facilities to no avail. He stole from stores, hocked his wife's wedding ring, drained their bank accounts, and stole over $25,000 from our church to feed his habit. After a DWI, six felony charges, and a nine-month state jail sentence, he only went deeper into his addiction.

While strung out and walking around downtown Dallas, a piece of paper blew onto his leg. He grabbed it and saw the words *GOD LOVES YOU.* Then and there, he surrendered to Christ and spent a year in a discipleship program. His faithful wife, Lauren, waited for him through all those years of hell while suffering through his addiction and praying (God bless all the steadfast spouses out there!). And as for the church he stole from? He was hired on as full-time staff on the facilities team and now literally has the key to every door in the entire church building. He is also both a leader and leader of leaders in our recovery ministry. Apart from Jesus, drug and alcohol addictions that run their course result in one or all of the following: rehab, jail, homelessness, death. They don't typically result in people becoming church staff, but no one has ever accused Jesus of being predictable.

So whatever your struggle has been, whatever has been part of your story, remember that you follow a God who makes all things new. In Christ, your past does not define your future; God does, period. So give it all to Him—the past, the pain, the loss, the struggles, the disappointments, the everything. He will use it all for your good and His glory, and the world will stand in awe.

This is not the end.
This is
THE BEGINNING
of a new life in Christ.
The way has been daily,
and freedom starts today.

PRAYER, ADDITIONAL RESOURCES, MERCHANDISE, AND INSTAGRAM

Visit freedomstartstoday.org for more stories of freedom, requests for prayer, additional materials, contact information, and merchandise to share this message of freedom with others.

Find encouraging verses, quotes, and stories of freedom on Instagram @john_a_elmore.

Suicide Prevention, Cutting, Struggling Hotline: 1800NEED HIM (1-800-633-3446) or TEXT (320) 345-3455 or chat at needhim.org.

Notes

Introduction

1. Martin Luther, "Ninety-Five Theses," in *Luther's Works*, vol. 31 (Philadelphia: Fortress Press, 1957), 25.

2. John Owen, *Of the Mortification of Sin in Believers* (Woodstock, Ontario: Devoted Publishing, 2017), 9.

Day 1 Sober 24 Hours

1. C. S. Lewis, *The Magician's Nephew* (New York: HarperCollins, 2001), 87.

Day 21 Get Off Your Ass

1. Martin Luther King Jr., "I've Been to the Mountaintop," speech, April 3, 1968, Bishop Charles Mason Temple, Memphis, TN, https://kinginstitute.stanford.edu/king-papers/documents/ive-been-mountaintop-address-delivered-bishop-charles-mason-temple.

Day 34 General Order #3

1. "Juneteenth," Texas State Library and Archives Commission, accessed April 26, 2020, https://www.tsl.texas.gov/ref/abouttx/juneteenth.html.

Day 35 Yellow Teeth

1. With gratitude to Timothy Keller for his powerful teaching on this topic from *The Freedom of Self-Forgetfulness: The Path to True Christian Joy.*

Day 38 Satan's Sinister Strategy

1. Jamie Ducharme, "U.S. Suicide Rates Are the Highest They've Been Since World War II," *Time*, June 20, 2019, https://time.com/5609124/us-suicide-rate -increase/.

2. Brianna Abbott, "Youth Suicide Rate Increased 56% in Decade, CDC Says," *Wall Street Journal*, October 17, 2019, https://www.wsj.com/articles/youth-suicide -rate-rises-56-in-decade-cdc-says-11571284861.

3. "Who Self-Injures," *American Psychological Association* 46, no. 7 (July/August 2015), https://www.apa.org/monitor/2015/07-08/who-self-injures.

About the Author

JOHN ELMORE is the senior director of pastoral care and director of recovery at Watermark Community Church in Dallas, Texas.

In December 2005, he put a loaded shotgun to his head and later had three doctors tell him he was dying of alcoholism. Now, over fifteen sober years later, he leads the world's largest weekly recovery gathering, called re:generation, where more than 1,200 people with every known sin struggle find healing in Christ.

Just months after sobriety, Elmore attended and was discipled at the Kanakuk Institute. He holds an MA in youth and family ministry from John Brown University and a ThM with honors in systematic theology from Dallas Theological Seminary.

John and his wife, Laura, have not had REM sleep since 2013, after having three kids in three years. They survive on coffee, takeout, and lots of prayer.

GET TO KNOW JOHN

Head to **freedomstartstoday.org**
for resources and more information about
John and re:generation.

 john_a_elmore

12-Step
Christ-Centered
Recovery

 re:generation™

Interested in learning more about re:generation? Head to
regenerationrecovery.org
for more information.

Connect with

Sign up for announcements about new and upcoming titles at

BakerBooks.com/SignUp

@ReadBakerBooks